How do we part with those we...
Life is an incredibly complicated journey. Loving with abandon is the best way to live, but also the most painful when it comes time to part, even for a little while. We have great hope because we know how to get to heaven. We know the parting is temporary, and that makes it bearable.

This is my husband's journey to eternity and the legacy he left behind. You would have loved him if you knew him. When we get to heaven, I will introduce you!

When a loved one passes away and you have done your best to meet his or her needs, the guilt you feel is usually false guilt. It is a lie Satan throws at us at a weakened time. Even if we have real regrets, Jesus died to cover up our mistakes with His blood. We are forgiven because He chose to pay for all our sins, knowing we would blow it from time to time. Nobody is perfect.

God said there is a time to be born and a time to die. He knows how and when we will die and does not alter it. So why do we blame God when it happens? He turns all things into good for those that love Him and are called according to His good purpose, even our losses.

When we lose someone, we have two choices, to become bitter or better, to draw closer to God or turn away from Him. He can help us with the pain and grieving if we lean on Him. If we blame Him, it is much harder to go through alone. God is not the author of death. He said Satan comes to steal, kill and destroy. Jesus came to give us a more abundant life.

Walk with me through phases of our life together and see how God molded this dear man into His image. He was on the Potter's wheel and sometimes in the fiery furnace, but he was never alone, and neither are you.

God gave me a gift of joy when Rog died. He made me so grateful that he was no longer suffering, and so happy for him, there was no room for much grief. I now know it was a special gift, and I am so thankful for it. I hope He gives you such a gift as well.

The Life of a Man of Integrity,

Determination and Faith

Every life is filled with interesting events, and Roger Parrott's was no different, but history always has lessons that can be learned, studying the lives of our relatives, since our grandchildren have his genes. I record a few events as a small legacy of a life very precious to me, my husband Rog, who passed away in 2010.

Rog's paternal grandfather was an orphan, raised in Angola, Indiana, and married Elizabeth, Roger's grandmother. (Her mother's name was Anna Ansbaugh.)

His maternal grandfather, Martin Meinhardt, was sent to America from Germany at the age of nineteen, and it is suspected his parents sent him here to escape the Prussian war, around the 1880-1890. He was apprenticed as a harness maker, but worked on the railroad as a foreman most of his life. Elizabeth died in about 1950. Martin was almost a hundred when he died in 1957 in St. Joseph, Missouri.

Rog's mom and dad, Emmett Mitchell, were the same age. Our son Thomas Mitchell and his son 'Mitch' are named after him. Our great grandbaby Emmett is named after Rog's middle name.

His mom was Leila Kathryn. Leila had a brother named Charlie who worked sorting mail in the caboose of a train. He was on the train when a bridge collapsed and the back half of the train went into the water with no survivors. Charlie was known to spend time in the engine compartment, so even though a body was found a week later with his ring on it, Leila refused to admit he was dead. She decided he must have sold his ring for money and used the tragedy as a way to get away from his estranged family. She searched for him for years after that. I don't think she ever came to grips with the fact he was dead.

Roger was born November 4, 1937 in St. Joseph, the youngest of three children. His sister Alice Marie, who now lives in Chama, New Mexico, was nine years older, and his brother Ron (who died in 2005) was six years above him in age. His dad had a college degree, and worked as a manager and buyer in large department stores.

He moved to Holland, Michigan when Rog was in third grade. That was a tough year for the poor little guy. The teacher decided he was a non-singer, and when the class sang, he was excused to do other things. He never tried to sing again! I often tried to urge him, but she destroyed his confidence. Then his mother was mortified to find Roger was put into speech correction class for talking southern! She soon became the PTA president, so those things could be done her way- the "right way".

His mom was a little spitfire German woman who knew how to get things done! She did everything well. She was a great housekeeper, cook, and seamstress. His dad was also very talented. Alice was a mezzo-soprano singer, and Dad made all her formals for performing on a treadle sewing machine.

Rog and his dad had little in common, so Ron took him under his wing, taught him everything mechanical, and taught him to hunt, which he did until he was in his fifties.

The family moved for a few years to Benton Harbor, Michigan where Rog had a chance to play football, but it was a disaster. He and his buddy were the only two "white guys" on the team, and they suffered merciless prejudice. He finally resigned from the team when some players deliberately broke his shoulder. He used to put it out of joint now and then to freak me out. The experience left him with a bad taste in his mouth for a long time.

At some point, Rog's dad contracted bacterial endocarditis, and became comatose. His mom refused to give up on him, and called a doctor from Holland, who drove down late one night to check on Emmett. The next morning, his dad was sitting in bed eating breakfast when Leila walked in!

The company he worked for in Benton Harbor, Michigan, replaced him while he was sick, so he woke up with no job! That had to be traumatic. They didn't give up, though. They invested all they had left after medical bills to buy an exclusive high-end clothing store back in Holland called "Town and Country," and made the back rooms into a connecting apartment.

While living there, Emmett had a stroke one time and went blind. A week later, however, he was completely well! Within a year, however, he got nephritis, kidney damage that resulted from massive doses of sulfa the doctor had to give him to wake him from the coma and heal his heart. With no health insurance or savings, they lost the business to bankruptcy. Then came more drama!

The Kidnapper
(Names changed to protect all of them)

When Rog was a senior in high school, he met Nita Z. She was so pretty, with long red hair and fair skin. Her sister Sherry was my best friend. Hank was the oldest. He must have been eighteen at the time. The three of them lived with their dad in a duplex in Holland, Michigan. My cousin Carol lived in the other side, so the three of us were together all the time.

A friend of Sherry's moved in with them named Irene, a tall slim dark-haired beauty with a tough exterior. She came from a broken family and Roland gave her a place to live, so he was her hero. Roland was very smart, and he was already making good money in the tool and die business. He bought the kids anything they wanted, and life looked like it was finally getting normal.

As Rog got to know the family, he started getting suspicious. He found that Roland, the kid's dad, had been in prison for several years for child molestation. Their mother had abandoned them as small children, and they had been raised in foster homes. The stories of abuse in those homes they shared with Rog disturbed him a great deal.

Over time, the story came out. Roland had been using all three girls for his purposes ever since he got custody of them and 'rescued' them from the foster homes. Rog tried to explain it to his friend Hank, who after many years of wanting a father and protector, turned on Rog, accusing him of being a trouble-maker. It broke Rog's heart, because Hank had been a close friend. He didn't realize he was jeopardizing Hank's new 'secure' lifestyle.

Rog didn't know what role to play in the drama. He hinted about it to his parents without telling the secret, which most likely had come to him from Irene, the chatterbox, but the parents' only advice was to get away from the family and avoid them. By then, he was committed to the girls and felt he was the only one who could help them.

At seventeen, he was financially independent, having learned a good work ethic with a paper route as a kid, and already had a steady job with a trucking firm. He owned a reliable car, and decided the only thing he could do was get the kids out of the state to Missouri and to his sister's house. She would know what to do.

He and Nita figured out a way to get Sherry and Irene out of the house in the night. With everything they had, the four of them sneaked out in the night when their father was asleep, walked to the corner, stowed their bags and quietly drove out of Holland.

They drove all night. When Roland realized they were gone, he called the police, who started a search for them. He knew Rog would be the rescuer, so all they had to do was trace his license number, put out an all-points-bulletin and pick him up, which they did.

The police put Rog in jail for kidnapping minor children. Sherry and Irene were fourteen or fifteen. His dad had to get him an attorney, which didn't make him happy, but his mom stuck up for him. It was quite a hassle, because the girls, feeling they were as guilty as their dad, didn't want to admit what Roland had been doing, so it looked like Rog was a liar. He felt betrayed by the whole bunch. Roland, of course, was back-peddling as fast as he could to stay out of jail again, accusing Rog of terrible things, and he was the most innocent of all! It appeared he stood completely alone, and it was not looking good for him.

A friend of our family, unknown to me, got involved. He was a parole officer and counselor named Avery Baker. He went to the jail and talked with Rog, did some investigating, and learned about Roland's record. He put the pieces together, got one of the girls to confess what was going on, and finally Rog was released. Avery kept pushing until he was able to get the girls back into foster care in Muskegon, and before too long, Roland was back in prison. Hank went away, and none of us ever heard about him again.

Rog knew me by association, and invited me to ride along in his red Ford convertible to visit Sherry at the foster home. That was my first contact with Rog, who later dated my other best friend. Then I got him!

Nita and Sherry both married over the next few years. I heard Sherry had a set of twins. I had tried to keep in touch, but the foster home parents wrote to all her friends and asked us not to contact her any more, so she could get on with a new life.

Now I understand it. I didn't then. Rog graduated from Holland High School in 1955 and we met shortly after that. He started dating my girlfriend Andrea...but she was still in love with another guy whom she had broken up with. She was using poor Rog to get even with her boyfriend. Andrea soon returned to him and got married.

Rog started buying motorcycle parts from me at Reliable and asked me for a date. Across the street from me, a neighbor, Mr. Doornbos, had an upstairs apartment for rent, and they were very hard to find, so Rog's family became my neighbors! It had no kitchen, but it was all they could afford. They had to wash dishes in the bathroom sink. It had to be so difficult to keep a good attitude suffering the shame of a bankruptcy, all the sickness, and then moving while knowing Emmett was dying.

It made his mom very nervous to have me so close, and for good reason. Rog and his family had been through an emotional war that was certainly not over, and he needed a friend. His mother tried to watch over him, but we secretly communicated in the night with flashlights and codes through the window across the street. She couldn't keep us apart.

A year later, December 29, 1956, we married. I was sixteen and he was nineteen.

We moved into a tiny apartment on 16th street above Central Hardware store for $35 a month. Rog and his mom both worked in the office of H.J. Heinz Company.

His dad had become bedfast, and died at home after several months of bleeding to death internally from nephritis, getting a transfusion nearly every day for several weeks. He passed away when our first baby was three months old. We got to the apartment in time to watch the paramedics carry his body down the narrow stairs on a stretcher. Two funerals were held-one in Holland and the final one in St. Joseph, Missouri.

Leila had an insurance policy on Emmett, and always made sure it was the first thing paid. When he died, she collected the hundred thousand, and even though she was not legally obligated to do so, she paid off the suppliers from the business, bought herself a darling little house on east 15th street near her job at Heinz, and bought a brand new pink and white Mercury sedan! She didn't have much left after that, but she always did the right thing. This mentality is not seen as much today.

She was very competent and confident, and dealt with life like a soldier. She used to come to visit us and if Davey was screaming, she just took him out of my arms, swaddled him snugly which seemed to help, and started rocking. He always quit crying when she came. She took us out for supper and to the laundromat every Saturday evening. It was a special treat. We didn't have money to eat out in those days. Rog ate breakfast with her every morning, so the kids and I could sleep in, before the kids were in school anyway. They worked together at Heinz doing bookkeeping.

Rog was quite a mechanic. He always amazed me with his abilities to fix anything. He and his brother rebuilt a motorcycle from scratch as a kid, and rebuilt a few cars in his day. When we married he had put a new engine in a 1952 Mercury that lasted us several years.

We lived in a tiny apartment on 16th street above Central Hardware until Dave was born, and moved into a huge apartment on 13th street, above a couple of alcoholics, Pansy and Slim Nicely. Slim used to get drunk and come upstairs to visit Rog. He terrified me when I was alone by pounding on the door and yelling for me to open the door.

1958 Herman Miller Hires Roger

I was so scared when Rog decided to get a new job. I feared it might not work out or they wouldn't hire him. Fears are such a waste of time. It was the best thing that ever happened to us both!

One time, pregnant with Tom, I put Davey in the buggy and tried going down the steps bouncing him down each step. I lost my footing, and the buggy, the baby and I tumbled all the way to the bottom, with him and the buggy landing on top of me! We could have been killed. What a stupid move that was. After lying there a while moaning while he screamed in terror, I regained my strength, and we had nothing broken, thank God.

As I said, we got married in 1956. I had no idea until we married that Rog had a severe case of psoriasis which covered his entire body with a heavy layer of thick scales. When he rolled over in bed, his skin would crack and bleed. His very dry skin allowed him to only shower in clear water twice a week.

Before Tom was born in 1959, Rog fell down our icy back steps, and landed on his tailbone. A cyst grew on it that had to be removed, which was not a minor operation. He had at least six inches of sutures. He always teased about being able to ride a motorcycle further than the rest of us because he had no tailbone.

His mom always discouraged us about not having any more children. I think she saw me as being too young, and we had enough on our plate, which may have been true. We always obeyed her.

A heart attack landed her in the hospital the night before her June first birthday in 1965. The night before, she dreamed her father appeared at the foot of the bed and knocked three times. Somehow, I think she knew she was going to die, because she had always said that dream came before every family death. How strange.

We got a call on her 65th birthday at seven in the morning. (Rob was born the next year on August 17, 1966.) She had a heart attack in 1965 and while in the hospital recovering, had another during breakfast and we got a phone call she had passed away. She had two funerals, one in Holland, and another in St. Jo, Missouri.

Travels and Children

We started out taking vacations when the kids were small with a big old army tent. We went to the beach every weekend in the summer. Then we bought a speedboat, and camped on Lake Michigan every weekend.

We got caught in a storm one night and nearly drowned getting the boat back into a port. Every summer, our leisure activities of weenie roasts, picnics, and water skiing, centered about Lake Michigan and its shoreline. Until we moved to Georgia when Dave turned seventeen, we lived in the dunes a mile from the lake, a wonderful playground. The kids built forts and dug big holes and jumped on their ground-level trampoline.

Rog and I had taken the boys, five and three, in the sixteen-foot ski boat to watch the Fourth of July fireworks and camp out in the open on the beach. We followed the shoreline for about ten miles north of the Grand Haven channel, and unloaded sleeping bags. After emptying supplies and family, Rog drove the boat out to waist deep water, anchored it, and waded back to shore. Settled in our sleeping bags under the sparkling stars and full moon, we listened to the gentle waves lapping to shore, giggling and sharing stories until we fell asleep.

Around three in the morning, Rog woke to a pounding in his ears, vibrating through his sand pillow. It increased in velocity until it disturbed him enough to realize his unique surroundings. His head was moist from the fog drifting in; the sound of wood slamming on a hard surface woke him with a start. The wind had come up without warning; black angry clouds obscured the full moon.

The rest of us slept on while Rog walked cautiously toward the banging sound. The waves were slamming the wooden boat, still anchored, onto a sand bar right beneath the surface.

He put on his swimsuit while trying to decide what to do. The waves sounded vicious but it was pitch black. Even if he knew how to swim, with the boat bucking like a bronco in darkness, he couldn't imagine how he could pull it onto the shore. He couldn't possibly, even with help, get it all the way out of the water, and he wouldn't be able to swim with the anchor into deep water in the wild sea. The boat would soon break apart and be lost. We were miles from a town, and would have to walk a long way in a storm with two little children.

It appeared the only logical, though dangerous, solution was to load us up and get safely inside the channel. Ten miles was not really that far, it seemed. Had he seen the ten-foot waves or known a tornado was meandering across the lake, he may have sacrificed the boat or tried to beach it and wait out the storm, but he didn't know.

By now, it was nearly four. A vague light rose in the east revealing the shadowy form, bobbing and pounding in the angry water.

He woke us with the news we had to get out of there as quickly as possible. We rolled up our gear while the kids stood like statues shrouded in sleep. It was now sprinkling, preparing for a downpour. Lightning revealed mountainous waves. Rog and I shoved our cold bodies into the wild waves, felt around for the anchor rope and dragged the boat off the sandbar.

He held the rope and I relayed the gear to him while the forlorn little boys stood trembling on the beach waiting for orders. David wondered if he was really awake. He had never seen the lake this wild. Though small and helpless, he gave the appearance of a brave soldier, holding Tommy's little hand. Tommy stood there with his eyes shut, still asleep, which explained why he wasn't screaming for his mommy.

Rog had an awful time getting into the boat without being run over. Climbing over the side was like mounting a galloping horse, but he made a lunge and landed on the floor with a thud. After throwing in the sleeping bags, with great trepidation I lifted Tommy up to him. As the boat plunged downward, he miraculously grabbed hold of him.

David was a bigger challenge. The waves knocked us both down under the surface before Roger snatched him and hauled him in. The wet clammy life jackets brought Tommy fully awake. Now the screaming began. It wasn't a dream any more! I frantically shoved the poor child under the deck for safety onto the sleeping bags. He miraculously fell back to sleep free from the storm.

I had no idea how I could get in that boat after so much exertion, but my life depended on it. I still cannot explain how I finally made it in. By then we had drifted back onto the sandbar; every second counted. Rog started the motor and it stalled. He tried again, and it fired, but the prop kept kicking up sand, slamming down on the sea floor.

The poor man was frantic. He screamed for me to get out and push us off the sandbar, but I was not about to get near a moving prop, and refused to get back in the water. Roger could see no other option in his panic and started yelling, "Get out and push! We are going to split in half!" I knew that was a really bad idea! It was a horrifying moment, with him yelling, the kids crying and the prop's high pitch as it rose in the air. Had I known God in those days, I surely would have prayed! But He knew me.

A huge wave settled the argument by turning the boat almost on its side, pouring in several gallons of water, but forcing it off the sandbar. It swung free and the prop grabbed something to work with.

Suddenly the sky split wide open like a huge bathtub had tipped over. Lightning exposed walls of water on both sides of us. David couldn't even scream; his tongue stuck to the roof of his mouth. Ten-foot waves leered at him above the deep valley where the boat caught a breath before climbing over the next mountain. I was busy bailing, and Rog was trying to find the direction to the channel.

We droned on for what seemed like hours from mountain to valley, seemingly making no headway. David was exhausted, clinging to the wooden bench, soggy and drained from the rain pelting his pale face. He was in shock, but knew if he released his grip, he would be hurled into the ferocious sea. He glanced up, hoping Dad could lend a hand before he collapsed, but one look and he knew there was nothing Dad could do to help him. He was on his own. Dad was desperately fighting to steer the nose into the waves to avoid being swamped.

David almost lost his grip when Dad shouted, "Land! I see the lighthouse! Oh, thank God!" I stopped bailing to look, and noticed David's terror. I dropped the bucket, grabbed him in my arms and held him tightly on my lap as he shook. Three hours had passed since we had left the beach.

The thunder and lightning abated and the rain slowed to a steady shower. The boat faithfully plodded toward the beckoning lighthouse. The mountains turned to foothills. We roared on into the protected channel. The boat was a third full of water. The red gas tank was floating, and debris sloshed around the floor. Totally exhausted, we clung to each other with relief.

The sun came out as we reached the coast guard station, where men stood waiting and pumped out the water. "What were you doing out in that storm?" one of them asked accusingly. What could we say? We had no access to a weather report and the evening had been mild. In any case, God had given us another day to celebrate life.

We discovered that a tornado had missed land, but several lives had been lost in that awful storm. The coast guard had a busy night. Thank God our precious little boys were given time to grow up and raise families of their own. Even better, we lived long enough to become Christians!

More Adventures

After Rog started doing people's taxes at night, we had enough money to go to Florida, so he bought a truck and camper that fit on the back, pulling the boat trailer behind it. We had wonderful adventures, spending two weeks every year in Florida.

Once we tied our terrier to a picnic table, went swimming in the ocean, returned to the camper and took off, forgetting poor little Buffy. It took two hours to return through heavy traffic to retrieve him. He was so happy he actually smiled.

Another time we got surrounded by dolphins swimming all around the boat! It was so exciting! We even saw a huge stingray swim right beneath us while we were stopped.

A Tour with Friends

Brazil was a dream come true. We hired a driver who took us into the interior through the jungle where we saw huge stalks of bananas and breadfruit being sold, and saw the palace and even met a princess. She was very old. Brazil had not had a king in a long time. We bought several pairs of shoes that were very cheap, and very expensive in the states. They had a McDonald's there where we bought one of everything they had for a dollar and sixty-five cents American money. That would not happen today.

Jumping Forward: A New Life Began

I became a Christian in 1973- a wild Bible-thumping miracle-loving enthusiast, and Rog didn't quite know what to think of it, though he had accepted Christ at nine. He said his whole class got 'saved' at the same time, and all were baptized one day. He was terrified of baptism because a friend had told him they hold your head down and say the

Lord's Prayer! He practiced holding his breath a few times in the bathtub but didn't do too well. He was relieved to find it wasn't true!

I was raised in church but never caught the teaching about being born again for some reason. I read all the books about evolution, 'Chariots of the gods,' Jeanne Dixon, Nostradamus, and all the rest. Nothing gave me peace. College didn't give me a purpose for my life. Anxiety increased, and my already poor coping mechanisms got worse.

It had never made sense to me. A man died two thousand years ago. He came back to life three days later. If I would just believe He rose, I could live with Him after I died. I heard the message for thirty-two years.

Finally in 1973 I was challenged to take a leap of faith, invite Jesus Christ to forgive my sins and come into my life and take over. I responded to the invitation. My 'reasoning mind' accused me of being insane. Rising above it revealed a realm I never imagined! To enter this realm, I had to leave reason behind. It was an experiment with the supernatural. The moment I prayed that prayer something happened to me.

This statement planted in me a sixth sense. How else can I explain such a drastic change? I was a different person. I finally understood spiritual puzzles that made no sense before and the words in the Bible made sense to me as never before. The change in me was complete and wonderful.

I told God I believed His Son Jesus died to purchase my soul. I told Him I believed Jesus was raised back to life here on earth, and asked Jesus to forgive me of everything I ever did wrong, and to accept me into the Kingdom of God. I felt so clean, pure, peaceful, and loved! God loves us so. All the lies we learned have blocked us from receiving His love.

Yes, we have been lied to, within and without. Until God's Spirit enters us, only by our invitation, we cannot understand this fact. If we deny Him and the Son He has sent us, He will deny knowing us at the end of our lives.

How thankful I am that I know where my soul will be when I leave this earth. Jesus said, "He that believes in Me will never die."

Rog was in northern Michigan deer hunting when all this went on. He took off hunting every year since we were married, going out west several times. He had some great adventures but we never recorded the details. Sorry.

When he came home, I just stood in the doorway, fully expecting him to see the light emanating from me! I didn't say a word. He greeted me with a hug but didn't notice a thing! I was shocked! I felt like a brand new different person, and he didn't bat an eye! When I told him about it, he said, "It is just another one of your fads. It will fade in time." How wrong he was.

I took the kids to church several years alone, when Rog wasn't taking them elsewhere. It was a busy life. I was in nursing school full-time, and Rog was doing income tax on the side at night. How we did it, I don't know. The family paid a price, of that I am certain. Children cannot raise themselves.

Leaping back again-stay alert now!

Our Beginning Together

I need to share this, though it is a different subject. I believe it has a lot to do with the direction Rog's life went. As I said,

I was sixteen and Rog was nineteen when we got married in 1956. I knew nothing about the organization he was in. Have you ever heard of the Freemasons? Neither did I, but I do now. Our church would not allow Rog to become a member because he was a mason, but nobody explained the reasons. They may not have even known. He sure didn't.

When we married, my father-in-law was a Freemason. His wife was in the Eastern Star, the women's section of Freemasonry. She never knew it is now considered by some to be a cult, and would have been horrified.

My husband became a Freemason and later the "Worshipful Master." (Can you imagine?) All our activities centered around Masonry and the Shrine. There was a lot of drinking and partying in the Shrine. I recall fearing he would become an alcoholic, and asking God to help. He contracted diabetes and could no longer drink. I guess that saved his life. It sure saved our marriage.

Roger renounced Masonry a few years ago when he nearly died from a heart problem. Friends shared an audio tape with him and he realized he had been deceived.

Our sons Dave and Tom also renounced their involvement with Demolay, the youth section. Getting in touch with anything occult alters one's path without a doubt, some more than others.

We have a friend who spent many years in Mormonism. When he learned the deception in Mormonism and the ties to Masonry, (Joseph Smith and his brother Hiram were Masons.) he began to study over a thousand books, including cryptic books for only Masons. He now speaks all over the country, mostly in churches. One day he went to a funeral and the hair on his neck stood up. He turned to see a group of men marching in with aprons on, wearing white gloves, and began chanting and breaking leaves over the coffin. Later his father said he wanted a Masonic funeral. "Over my dead body!" our friend said. His father later renounced Masonry and died a Christian.

It began with the stonemasons in Solomon's time. They learned secret handshakes and signs to show other masons they belonged to the craft of stonemasonry, but nothing more. Spiritual Masonry began much later.

The first Grand lodge met in England in 1717. Masonry was involved in the French and American Revolutions, and a conspiratorial part of America's history. Many in the first Congress were Masons. The Declaration of Independence was written on a Masonic white lambskin apron. Masons designed the Congressional Medal of Honor, which has on it a pentagram, the most powerful satanic emblem. The statue of Liberty was a gift from Masons in France to the American Masons. It is filled with occult symbols.

Initiates are told this is a brotherhood organization that allows all religions to join, and that it is not a religion, but it definitely is. It is not Christian, by any means. The secret identity of God is Jabulon, and stands for Jehovah, Ba'al, and Osiris, the Egyptian sun god. The swearing-in ceremony and the rituals make this a religion in honor of demons. The key demon is the Goat of Mendes or Baphomet.

When a Mason receives his apron, he is told it should be his covering when they stand before the great white throne judgment of God. They don't realize this is the judgment of the damned!

The sacred word learned at a certain level of the Scottish rite is Abbadon. This is the king of hell, Satan.

Blue Lodge members are sworn to keep brethren's secrets, murder and treason excepted. Royal Arch Masons are sworn to protect even murder and treason. Imagine going to a court of law and expecting a fair trial when the judge is upholding first his oath to the Masons. If you hear of a crazy court case that is not going fairly, you might examine the roots of Masonry.

Scriptures and Bible teachings are sometimes quoted in Masonry but the name of Jesus Christ is omitted.

Those that partake of only the first thirty-two degrees of Masonry, though they have made terrible vows, have not taken communion of the dead, drinking wine from a human skull, as in the 33rd level of the Scottish rite.

Once they study and pass the 32nd degree, they may go into the Shrine-for a price, of course. This oath includes an oath that says, "May Allah, the god of Arab, Moslem, and Mohammedan, the god of our fathers, support me..." Allah is not God the Father of Jesus Christ! It is a deity entombed in a building in Mecca where Islam worships it. No Christian can submit to or swear allegiance to this demon god, Allah. Many

Christians are unaware that Allah is not the God of the Christians.

Why is the Fez they wear red? The Muslims butchered forty-five thousand people in the city of Fez that refused to bow to Allah. They dipped their white hats in the blood of the Christian martyrs.

If families of Masons are having sickness or any other cursed things bothering them, they need to examine their relationship with God. He is a jealous God, and has a right to be. He gave His only Son to save us. Nobody else deserves our allegiance. Masonry brings a curse into families to the third and fourth generation of those that have turned from God. God honors repentance from the heart and forgives sin.

There are many Masons sitting in churches unaware that they have been disloyal to God. They simply have been deceived. It does not help to condemn them, but pray and share what you know to be true if they will listen. Many great articles are found on the internet. The above information came from one called, "Freemasonry and the Church" by Ed Decker with permission.

Another New Beginning!

By this time, Rog was working in the accounting department at Herman Miller Furniture before it got really famous for office furniture. He was instrumental in several major changes, and an important asset to the company. In 1977 he was promoted to Director of Southern Operations in charge of a factory built in Roswell, Georgia. We had built a beautiful home in the Lake Michigan dunes when Rob was two, and sold it after eight years, moving to Alpharetta, Georgia, where the kids enjoyed the life of Riley in Rivermont Subdivision, a golfing community with all the amenities.

Life was good. We went to Europe that year for six weeks with Rog's sister and her husband Johnny. Rob, age 11, was sent to Michigan that time. Tom and Dave were alone, and 'borrowed' our pickup truck and drove it into a ditch. He said he had to avoid hitting a dog in the road. The police had it hauled to an impound yard. Tom stole it back, afraid he would get in trouble with his dad, and was put in jail for 'stealing' our own truck. A neighbor, an influential airline pilot, bailed him out and arranged it so there was no consequence.

When we moved to Georgia, we put Rob in a Christian school twenty miles from home. I had completed three of four years of nursing school for a BSN, but my credits would not all transfer, so I had to backtrack a bit. I dropped my major down to an RN program and returned to school. Dave had quit college in Northern Michigan and moved with us. Tom was a senior in High School.

The Unforgettable Cruise

Rog and I were married December 29, 1956, and thirty years seemed like a good anniversary to really celebrate. A few days before Christmas, we stopped by a travel agency to check on a Caribbean Cruise. The only thing left on such short notice was a Greek ship called the Amerikanis, and the only cabin left was on the bottom floor next to the engine, for $1130 a person from Miami. Supposedly all expenses were included. That was our first surprise! Nonvolunteer tips, drinks, tours and more were all very expensive.

I must say that it was ultimately the most wonderful trip in the world, in spite of all the complaints we started out with. None of them dampened our spirits, however. We were so excited to take our very first cruise. The trip to the Virgin Islands began on December 30. 1986. We flew to Miami, and then to San Juan, Puerto Rico, arriving in the early evening. What a thrill it was to walk off the plane in Miami after leaving a terrible snowstorm in Grand Rapids, Michigan.

Rog's boss sent us flowers to greet us in our room! We were not upset to find the bed on the ship was only a bit larger than a twin, or that the sink didn't work, but when we found the shower didn't work, either, we were concerned. TV was only in Spanish, or some other language. The drawers stuck shut, the bed was hard and lumpy, the blanket was thin and narrow and the pillows were flat! The alarm clock failed to go off so we missed a landing in St. Thomas. I got a canker sore on my tongue. Rog's shaving kit got sopped because the sink leaked. The faucet wouldn't stay on for us to brush our teeth. We weren't surprised when we had to wait a half an hour for the elevator, so we often chose to walk five flights to the deck. We just took our stuff with us and stayed there until bedtime.

Our first dinner on the boat took so long we missed the orientation and slides. The boat left late due to lost luggage, our keys were missing and we had to sit in our cabin awaiting them so we missed going out to explore San Juan until dark. Then we were warned not to wander around.

Our luggage did not show up for hours, so we had no comfortable shoes or clothing to wear the first day. A change of clothing was required three times before we got our suitcases!

We had a bit of trouble getting to sleep when at night we travelled from port to port with the engine roaring in our ears, but we had been warned ahead of time. The first morning we missed breakfast completely because they verbally announced it for 8:30, but actually served it at 8:00. By 8:30 they were closed!

The troubles mounted, though, when we were assigned seating at every meal with strangers whom had nothing in common with us. Ron drank too much, maybe because his wife had left him after 24 years for another man, and took their four kids with her. Ron and Linda, not married to each other, gave us a blow by blow description of every night's escapades, including things that should never be mentioned. They were buying drugs in ports and shocking us with the lack of concern about being arrested. Noreen, 35, was single by choice and pregnant from a sperm donor. Her friend Marsha, who had two small children, came along. It came out in conversation that Noreen was lesbian, but Marsha, married, seemed pretty normal. It was confusing.

Our waiter George, from the Philippines, worked seven days a week for eighteen hours a day! He had five children and had not been home in years. He has to work to support his family, and sends home most of his pay. His eleven year old son was killed in a car accident when he was working in Saudi Arabia. We don't know what a tough life is!

One day we got off the ship and onto the Jolly Roger, a "pirate" ship. Rum punch freely flowed, into almost everyone, including children whose parents had sent them off for a "good time." They got drunk and one was hauled off the ship on a stretcher, dead drunk at twelve. Drugs were being sold at the edge of the beach behind the tree line. People were all excited with their 'treasures.' I was abhorred!

We took it all in stride until I started getting seasick, about the second day, because we started having dinner in the dining room and they were moving at the time. I couldn't take it. I finally broke down and went to the infirmary for something to stop vomiting. The doctor said he didn't have my medical records so he couldn't give me anything! Thank God a man who overheard gave me an atropine patch. After three days of being sick I started doing better and we went to the movies on board and I even went swimming.

The pool was unique. It was a flat-sided round tub about twelve feet across and about twelve feet deep, but the water was about four feet deep in the bottom. I was the only one swimming. I had to climb down a long ladder on the side. By the time I got down there, I got claustrophobic and had to get right out again.

I took Dramamine at breakfast one morning and went sound asleep until after lunch! I watched a movie in the afternoon called "FX" and Rog went to the Follies.

We landed on the island of Guadeloupe. We took a tour for $22 each to the rain forest. The guide told us a volcano puffed a bit in 1976 and everyone panicked and ran to Grand Terre. They speak Creole, French and English, and the population was 350,000. They have 200 inches of rainfall in the mountains! (In contrast, Israel had 3" a year.)

They raise sugar cane, bananas, African tulips, yams (not sweet potatoes), gigantic Irish potatoes, coconuts, hibiscus, poinsettia, grapefruit, oranges and lemons. The leaves of a creamy fruit called Sala sapa help you sleep.

Other crops are huge plantains, green figs, cinnamon, a chili plum tree, coffee beans, papaya, avocadoes, passion fruit, star fruit, guinabana, and a white gum tree. Its bark is a gun that they burn as incense to keep away evil spirits. They also have almonds, tangerines, chestnuts, mangoes, chutney, breadfruit trees, yoghurt, and alamonda-yellow flowers that are very poison. Egrets ride on the cows' backs. A royal palm grows to 110 feet. They have tiny black goats and fighting cocks in cages. They had one Catholic Church, wild orchids all over, and no dangerous animals or mosquitoes.

Two nights they put on shows while we travelled, and they were really great, except that one performer lost her footing and broke her leg. That put a damper on the show!

One noon there was a wonderful ice sculpture and show. We watched this guy shape a dolphin out of ice. It was really beautiful. The food was so good, I gained ten pounds in a bit over a week!

In the ports, kids were diving for money we threw overboard. They sure had guts. The water near shore was so filthy. We didn't go on any other tours because the price was outrageous. Hardly anyone spoke English, so mainly the people we could talk to were our table-mates, which wasn't any treat. If Rog had allowed it then, I would have been sharing Jesus stories with them. We weren't quite there yet.

We still had a good time in the warm weather, shopping at the islands, going to movies and lying in the sun. Not knowing there was anything better, we thought it was great. Only looking back do I realize why I never envied anyone for going on a cruise!

Friday we missed breakfast again, so we walked down to see a submarine called Atlantis. Rog's hat flew away, and we failed to catch it. The buffet by the pool was yummy at noon. Later I took disco lessons, Cha-cha and Sa-sa with Dierdre. I was her only student!

The next morning we got up in time for breakfast on the deck, got to Antigua by nine, and taxied to Jolly Roger's flatboat to an island. On the way, rum flowed freely to all ages. One little girl got smashed to the gills and was not walking. All the booze was free. They had a plank, a rope swing, a swimming beach and a limbo contest. If I had children, I would have really been worried. Nobody seemed to care. A long clothesline was strung up on the beach with clothes to sell. Noreen told me the natives were selling and using cocaine and crack in the jungle right behind the clothes. Sounded like Ron really liked the stuff. No wonder Linda said she had her hands full with him. Ron told a well-endowed woman how gorgeous her breasts were! She had attached herself to a loser, but he connected with a person able to destroy his ego quickly. Oh, my. Can't repeat things she said about him to us.

Marsha's most exciting feat was to steal her last piece of silverware, a spoon, to complete her place setting to take home. Her 87-year-old grandma asked her to do that for her. A priest talked to us about the difficulties of being surrounded by all this materialism and of the fifty starving people in his parish.

The scenery was out of this world. Snorkeling over a wreck was cancelled due to a storm that had destroyed visibility. A bug hit me right in the eye on the way to the ship, and my vision remained blurry all day but later improved. The seasick patch worked wonderfully the whole trip. I was so grateful for that man who gave it to me.

That evening was costume and Caribbean dress night and party at 10:30 p.m. The night before they had a fabulous show! The first young gorgeous gal sang her heart out, dressed in a white skirt, silver shoes, and a white and silver blouse. The second singer wore a short tight white skirt and a green dark shirt, and the third wore a light green jumpsuit with a silver jacket knotted at the waist. The fourth looked like Carmen Miranda. They were fantastic singers.

Before the party, we watched the sun set behind the mountains outlined in black beneath a brilliant gold sun, the balmy breezes massaging our arms. It was quite an adventure, perhaps not perfect had we known there were better ones, but we didn't so we just had a magnificent time. We were not at all discouraged over the imperfections. Amazing when you don't know any different, how little it bothers you.

What would I have changed if I could? The food was exquisitely served and very healthy, activities galore, air conditioning inside was just right, very friendly staff, waited on hand and foot, clean sheets every day and the room was often cleaned through the day if needed. They had lots of fat towels, and no tipping until the end. I would have liked to snorkel some.

All the Caribbean islands appear very poor and dirty. People threw the divers all sorts of things besides money and food.

I would love to go on a Christian tour, but this was clean, no dirty jokes, few drunks around, good warnings about taxies and dangers of every sort, and they had bingo and every morning they had Mass.

What have I seen? Jellyfish, steel bands that were outstanding, breathtaking sunsets, and I had a chance to share miracles and the love of Jesus with many people.

We arrived back in San Juan at 7 a.m. January 5, 1987. The rain was somewhat depressing. We had to let all the foreigners get off the ship first, which took a long time. All the burdens of the world crept back into our lives. We had to shake them off again! That is why I wrote this memoir. Memories are precious.

Bikers Are Regular People!

My dad owned a store that sold a huge variety of things, including motorcycles. On almost our first date Rog put me in front of him on his big Harley and let me steer! I slammed right into a car that turned in front of us, smashing my ankle. Rog flew off. The cycle was in rough shape and Rog got a ticket! Great way to start dating.

He bought me a Honda after we married and years later we joined the Christian Motorcyclists Association (CMA). We drove the bikes to a rally in Hatfield, Arkansas that was awesome! How can I tell you how much God loves you...just as you are! He reads your mind and your heart.

Some of the people we spent a week with came from the most difficult and abusive lifestyles you can imagine! There are ex-convicts, some have murdered, some had many illicit relationships, and some have been full of hate and anger. God forgave them all, and welcomed them all into His kingdom. It is so heartwarming to see the extent Jesus goes to reach us and change us.

Nearly a thousand people registered for this rally, which consisted of motorcyclists from all over the country. What a sight to see all those little tents as far as the eye can see. An entire town was all laid out in block form.

CMA has one purpose. We are taught evangelism to share the gospel with bikers everywhere. Most of the members are in ministry to unsaved bikers, and had some very amazing stories to share. I collected the stories with a camcorder so I could record them accurately when I got home. You can find them in my book, Motorcycle Miracles, on Amazon.

Bikes have been a big part of our lives.

I Waited Sixteen Years for this

In 1988, God used Mark Dees as an instrument to draw our family into a deeper walk with God, praying often with our grandkids. He invited Rog and me to dinner one night, and we had a great time until he led the group of about twenty to sit in a circle and share their testimonies. It made me very nervous, because Rog would think I set him up for embarrassment. Before it was his turn, though, Mark changed the format and told us to grab a partner and pray for each other. He chose Rog. We were all praying, and suddenly Mark announced that Roger had just received the Baptism in the Holy Spirit.

I just assumed another Roger was there, and looked around to see him, and it was MY Roger! Mark had prayed with him in his wonderful way, and my precious husband was truly born again and filled with God's Spirit. He was glowing. I knew it was real, because the next day he was with me in church, and even started tithing, the very first day! Life got better and better.

He did a lot of work at the church with his buddy Morey Arnold, helping whenever he was free. He quietly went about his business, but was a strong influence of integrity for those that knew him.

Yes, we are very blessed.

Rog sent me to Israel with my church friends in the late eighties, and my parents went along. I went two more times, and Rog went along. It was a highlight of our lives.

Israel cannot even be described adequately. It is our real home. We all wept when we left Tel Aviv for home. Magnificent! Flowers everywhere! Music is in the air all over. Musicians play in the streets, accordions, violins, you name it. Men with sons on shoulders do the Israeli dances right in the streets.

Children are everywhere, selling trinkets. Everyone has to take a camel ride, and take care they don't spit on you. I swam in the Dead Sea where you cannot get your feet on the bottom because the water is so salty that you float. You can float out where it is fifty feet deep, look down and see huge boulders the size of a house! When you get out, you must rinse at the shower or you turn pure white from the salt.

The people are so very kind, and Arabs and Jews get along, totally unlike the portrayals on the news. The food is wonderful. Netania is a town on the Mediterranean, the only place in the world where the rocks on the beach are shaped like hearts!

Back Home Again

Rog worked hard, and he supplied our financial needs. He was baptized at nine with his class, but we didn't attend church much after we married. I was raised in church, too, but lost sight of who Christ was until I couldn't answer correctly when people asked me if I knew Him.

Rog was raised with a firm hand and a rod. I was gently raised and could not imagine such a thing, so I got in the way when he tried to discipline. We were on opposite ends of the spectrum with childrearing. I was too lenient and I believed he was too strict. We were both guilty of making wrong decisions. Some of mine were not protecting helpless vulnerable children and standing up for them. I could have done it in a way that would still provide a united front, but take the guilt feelings from the kids for things they were not responsible for.

If we really obeyed God when we were younger, we would have treated our children and each other so differently. Very likely, Rog's desire later on to bail the kids out when they have troubles was a result of past events that he regretted, but did not consciously acknowledge. I know he loved them a great deal, but could not verbalize it. Instead he gave them things. (It would be lots cheaper to say I love you-ha-ha.)

What does God teach us about love? *If I speak in the tongues of men and of angels, but have not love, I am only a resounding gong or a clanging cymbal. If I have the gift of prophecy, and can fathom all mysteries, and all knowledge, and if I have a faith that can move mountains, but have not love, I am nothing. If I give all I possess to the poor and surrender my body to the flames (as a martyr for the faith), but have not love, I gain nothing.*

Love is patient, love is kind. It does not envy, it does not boast; it is not proud. It is not rude, it is not self-seeking. It is not easily angered, it keeps no record of wrongs. Love does not delight in evil, but rejoices with the truth. It always protects, always trusts, always hopes, and always perseveres. Love never fails.

Open Door Policy

This story shows what Rog was like. God led him even when he was unaware of it. I wish I had kept a journal of all the people who stayed with us over the years. It made life so interesting. Never a dull moment!

Rog traveled a lot, so in about 1993 I got a job working in a Christian bookstore. The customers were like family and I enjoyed it.

One night I had a vivid dream about a pretty young woman living in the ghetto on the street. She was being chased all night long by various people with knives, broken bottles and even guns. After watching her escape one captor after another, just before I woke up, God spoke to me. "If each of My children took in just one person who had no home, there wouldn't be any out there." I shuddered, wondering if He was asking this of me.

We had an open door policy at our house nearly since we married. Cousins, friends' kids going to college and even old neighbors lived with us from time to time. Two of our children returned home after their marriages failed and our grandchildren spent a lot of time with Gran. I loved it.

I was visiting with my boss the next morning. "I had this vivid dream about a poor woman with no place to live. She was frantic, trying to stay alive out there." As I was talking, a woman limped into the bookstore. I glanced up at her face and almost lost my breath! It was the face in my dream! "May I help you?" I asked, wondering what it all meant.

She proceeded to choke up as she told me her terrible situation. "I was caring for this woman, and she died yesterday! The family informed me I had to move out immediately. I had been like family, I thought, caring for her for over a year. I was devastated by their sudden rejection. I packed up as fast as I could and got in my car, embarrassed at my misconception. I have been riding around all morning, wondering where to turn."

My heart went out to this pretty woman in her thirties. Her dark hair hung over her face, covering her beautiful brown eyes. "May I use your bathroom, please?" she asked. I pointed toward the restroom and watched with compassion as she dragged one leg behind the other as though she was lame.

Suddenly the dream came back. "If My children would take in one person..." I realized it was God getting my attention. While she was out I prayed, "Lord, I need a sign this is from you. Please give Rog your answer when I call him in New York City." He was on a business trip. I called him and told him about the woman but not the dream. Without ever meeting her, he did something totally out of character for him. "You talk to her. Invite her to live with us free as long as she wants." This is my cautious husband who would always allow people to stay with us, but would never invite a stranger in. I knew it was God!

Susie and I talked for a while and I asked her a lot of questions. She opened her heart to me. "I was married to a wealthy man. We used to have a few drinks together before and after we had our two children. It got to be sort of a problem for me, but more than that, I came down with multiple sclerosis. My husband saw the handwriting on the wall and knew he did not want to be saddled with me. Being rich, he was able to hire the best attorney. He made it look like I had a more serious drinking problem than I had, and had a detective take pictures of me staggering around to show the judge. Before I knew it, he had custody of my children and had cut me off completely, with no family, no support and no hope. I went from riches to rags in a very short time, and found myself living in my car, eating wherever I could find food."

"How in the world did you even keep your car going?" I asked, needing to know the whole story, which I was getting, but had no way to verify it. Who would lie about such a thing and why? She didn't know I was thinking of taking her in. I was not afraid about it since I had evidence God was asking it of me.

"I finally got jobs caring for older people, but nobody paid me much because of my MS." She never told me whether she got government help, but I found later that she had some money in the bank.

At that point I asked if she wanted to stay with me until she could find something better. She wept again, and hugged me. Soon she was living in my house, and remained for three years.

She would not let me feed her, and was painfully thin. Every morning she drove away in her car and returned in the evening, never talking much. She stayed in her room most all the time when she was home. She was Catholic, and went to church a lot. One day she came home early from church. I asked if something happened, and got a clue about her mental status.

"I realized they were pumping poison through the ventilators and I got real scared I might not get out before it overcame me, so I got out of there."

"What makes you think it was poison?" I asked. She answered with a story I can't even repeat that revealed she had an emotional problem with paranoia and reality. The next morning I followed her to see where she went every day. I found she was just sitting in her car in the grocery store parking lot doing nothing. I started fearing she would die of starvation if we couldn't get her some help.

She refused to answer questions about her family. I got so concerned I hired a detective to help me find them. I established a phone relationship with her daughter she had not spoken with since the girl was eleven. One evening the daughter's husband called my home and asked to speak with Susie.

Susie never asked me how he found her, so I didn't tell her. He called every Wednesday evening for almost a year, and she seemed to enjoy the calls. One day I called him and told him we were moving out of town and had no place to keep her with us. He offered to bring her home to live with him and her daughter.

I started letting her know we were thinking of moving. Soon the For Sale sign went up. About that time her son-in-law invited her to come live with them, and her daughter even got on the phone and they began to establish a relationship. Lots of prayers had gone up over three years, some for her deliverance from paranoia, and others for her disease.

We had a Bible study at my house one evening and the girls surrounded Susie and invited her to join us. She had started trusting me just a little by then, and had even eaten a few meals with me. That evening as we prayed, Susie shared a bit of herself- enough for us to intervene in prayer.

She received deliverance that night from spirits that had oppressed her since her divorce, and we led her to repeat the prayer for salvation, just in case she might have missed it. The next morning, Susie did not climb down the stairs on her bottom like she had to because of MS, but she walked down every step! I wept watching her! God had healed her legs. From that day on, Susie also ate three meals a day! Her communication improved and she became completely logical and even uplifting. I discovered she actually had a sense of humor and a delightful personality!

A month later, she put her car up for sale because it was old and not running any more. We packed all her belongings in my car and took off for Virginia to meet her daughter face-to face for the first time in many years. It was a rather stiff reunion, but a beginning. They shook hands like strangers, such a sad statement from years of pain. I hugged her, emptied her belongings and returned home.

Why won't this vacuum slide under the bed? Getting on my knees, I peeked under

Susie's bed after she had left. It was so full of candy wrappers, I had to dig them out with a rake! No wonder she had no appetite for food and looked so vitamin-deprived. I guess that was the only thing that she liked any more.

Susie wrote to me once a year for a long time, telling me she was so happy, living with her grandchildren around her. She even gained twenty pounds and was feeling very well. Her daughter finally knew the truth, and the truth set them both free.

John 10:10 (KJV) ^The *thief cometh not, but for to steal, and to kill, and to destroy: I am come that they might have life, and that they might have it more abundantly.*

The gaps in the story are not to confuse you, but to hit the high notes so you won't be bored! I could tell you about these in-between years, but the book would be so very long!

1997 was quite a year!

Rog had rheumatic fever as a child, and as a result has lived with a damaged aortic heart valve since then. In January of 1997, soon after his retirement, he fell down an entire flight of stairs, temporarily lost his memory, broke some ribs and had a concussion, and severely damaged that heart valve.

The doctor gave him two months to live without surgery. So he had the valve replaced and had two heart by-passes in the process, since he was being opened up anyway. Now he must take Coumadin the rest of his life, requiring him to have blood tests twice a month. This, in addition to poking his finger twice a day, puts a lot of stress on his poor system.

The heart surgery was probably the most serious thing he has survived. He got through it very well, saying the worst part was being on a breathing machine that was set too high for his lungs. He nearly lost his mind that first night after surgery, and I was not allowed to be with him as the nurse had promised. Rog was frantic almost to a frenzy, but he was tied down and couldn't move or speak. Finally, he said, a black man came in and bathed him, and calmed him down.

In the morning as soon as the vent was removed, Rog told the nurse about the man. She said she was the only person that had been allowed in his room all night and there were no black men of that description working there! Yes, angels certainly do exist!

The amazing thing was that Rog had no pain whatsoever following that surgery! His legs were cut to his knees, his chest was cut top to bottom, and he suffered not a moment of pain! He refused the pain medication, he walked the very first day, and has recovered remarkably well.

We didn't realize his absence of pain was unique until the six week checkup. We were sitting in the waiting room visiting with others who had the same surgery and they were all still suffering many weeks later! Wow.

So this is the story up to today. God has given us hope of eternal life with no pain, no sorrow, and no tears. We look forward to this, but we are already in His Kingdom. He has told us we have at our disposal healing, deliverance, and much more…on this earth, in this life.

We have seen many unexplainable miracles, and we know God can do anything. We have to ask, and we have to believe Him with all our hearts. Sometimes we have to fight our own minds which refuse to cooperate. Now and then, we must fight the lies of the devil himself, who comes to steal, kill, and destroy…but Jesus came to give us life more abundantly.

We had a very active interesting life. I can't say in those earlier days of Christianity we had benefitted others a lot, but did what everyone around us did, going to banquets, going on vacations, working hard and minding our own business. We kept things in order, bought and sold, had marriages babies and funerals and all that entails an average family.

Later in 1997

I went to Michigan to be with my sister while she had brain surgery on her pituitary gland tumor. When I returned in two weeks, Rog had lost at least twenty-five pounds, and he looked like a war refugee! His clothes hung on him, his color was awful, and he was in bad shape! He had attributed it to a 'protein fast' he had started when I left, but this was much more severe a result than he should have expected. Back to the doctor we went.

He was put under anesthesia, and a camera was sent down his throat right into his pancreas. A duct was no longer functioning, and he produced no more digestive enzymes. He was starving to death.

So now he must take enzymes with all his meals. He is doing much better, and his weight is normal, but he was left with some intestinal ulcers (found recently in another scope), and lots of gas pain. Every so often, he gets severe stomach pain for a few days due to chronic pancreatitis or the ulcers.

November 11, 1999

Rog has been up half the night as usual. I do believe I live in a state of denial about his health, and expect so much of him, simply because he never complains. I am able to ignore his condition for this reason. What is his condition?

Most of the problems, it seems, began with a broken foot bone at the age of twenty-seven. He went to a podiatrist to have it looked at, and the man performed experimental surgery, I believe illegally, in his office. He opened Roger's foot under local anesthesia! He took a saw and cut his bone right in half while Rog watched! Within a couple weeks he had diabetes- Type I. His pancreas had stopped functioning entirely, our doctor told us, from the shock. No, we could not sue the doctor. He had died.

He was told he has Type II diabetes, as the Type 1 left for five years and later returned as Type 2. That is a story in itself. God took it away supernaturally.

For many years since I became a Christian at age thirty-two, I prayed sixteen years for my husband to come to church with me. I love him very much. He is a good man.

We have seen many miracles in his life. He had Type I insulin dependent diabetes five years when I got saved. One night, the Holy Spirit woke me, and spoke clearly to me. He said if I would lay my hands on Roger, He would heal him of diabetes. I was a new Christian, but had already been healed of a severe back problem, and I knew God could do anything.

So without waking him, I did just that. I thanked God for healing him, and fully expected by morning, he would be well. He went to work with no evident changes in his condition. But a week later, he took his regular insulin shot, and suddenly his blood sugar plunged! He ended up, I believe, at the hospital. He was told not to take any more insulin, because it might kill him! His pancreas had begun to function normally! It was 1974.

I was beside myself with elation, but Rog thought I had simply lost my mind, and was giving God credit for what he himself had done. He had lost weight, stayed on the diet, and was very diligent, so he assumed he had healed himself. The doctor hinted it might have been a 'honeymoon' period. They last, at the most, for two years. His lasted five years, and he ate everything a diabetic would not dare eat.

It has been said that stress results in a cycle of breakdowns, which we have surely seen in his life. I have never even had surgery, and have never been seriously ill! I can't even relate to the suffering this dear man has gone through. It is easy for me to ignore it and pretend it is no big deal.

Close Encounters

Rog's diabetes remained healed until the day I had been in Michigan with Rob for a week visiting my parents. Rob was twelve, so it was 1978. Rob and I nearly lost our lives in a mountain accident pulling a huge boat on an inadequate size trailer. Rog came to help us get home and repair things. He had just taken his first shot of insulin in five years. (It seems every time I leave town, he gets sick with something.)

God answered so many prayers during this time. He saved us from dying in the car/boat accident, which is quite a story.

My dad asked me to drive his car pulling a boat from Holland, Michigan to Georgia for a customer.

I agreed, so he scrounged around for a hunk of wire to tie up the Buick's dilapidated muffler, found some illegal license plate for the trailer, and plugged its brake line into the car. In his haste, however, he didn't tell me the only trailer on hand to carry this twenty-seven foot Seacamper houseboat was 'way below capacity to haul this enormous burden, and forgot to advise me to tighten the wheels' lug bolts every hundred miles during the trip from Michigan to Georgia. *What tiny wheels*, I noticed, but never considered why.

My dad was a forgetful but lovable businessman who often took chances conservative people would never consider, especially this one, gambling with our very lives for the sake of a boat sale. Dad's escapades have become legend. We still tell entertaining stories of his antics at parties. (I hope he is laughing up there in heaven.) Usually his risky decisions turned out all right, but this time I may not have been here to tell it if God had been hard of hearing.

I took off that hot July day with my twelve-year-old co-pilot, our son Rob. I didn't mind driving instead of flying back, since he offered to pay me a healthy bonus to deliver it. I had never pulled such a giant before, but was impressed that Dad trusted me with his treasure. Two sins are greed and pride. I was guilty of both.

    We woke the next morning after a pleasant night in the elegant new houseboat, parked in a Kentucky RV park. After buying breakfast, we headed to the Tennessee Mountains. The trailer was struggling to stay straight behind the car. *Maybe I am just oversteering. I have to relax a bit,* I thought.

    Climbing the first high mountain was difficult for the Buick; we finally got to the top, but trying to keep control as the boat shoved the car down the steep slope was quite another story. Our speed kept increasing in spite of pumping the brakes, and the smell of rubber warned me to scan frantically for a ramp where trucks can coast upward off the road when they can't slow down.

    I realized with sudden horror that I'd lost control when the car suddenly began bucking and swaying across the four-lane highway. Rob said later he knew we were going over the cliff and die a horrible death, but was too scared to speak. Too panicked to pray, I simply screamed at the top of my lungs, "Jesus!"

Without my assistance the car, heading for the ravine, as if shoved by some gigantic hand, spun completely around toward the median, and some large object flew over the hood. Fifty feet of car and trailer abruptly stopped, spanning the entire highway. Rob and I braced for the inevitable crash as vehicles came flying around the curve.

The car stalled, but incredibly it started just in time for me to drag the trailer to the median inches from traffic whizzing around the curve. We didn't yet realize the trailer axle had cracked almost in half, and the flying object was a tire! The boat loomed in the air like a sheltered queen on her throne, untouched. The only immediate visible damage was a badly twisted trailer hitch.

A trucker, expecting a wreck, was ready to help and stopped nearby. He told me, "I saw the wheels wobbling, and I knew you were in trouble." The kind man separated my car from the trailer and handed me the twisted hitch parts. Rob and I headed for the nearest town a few miles off highway 75.

After I called my husband from a gas station in Lake City, Tennessee, an eavesdropping stranger warmed my heart by offering to weld my broken hitch and repair it at no charge. A policeman in the gas station gave me a stern order, "You are required to place triangular warning reflectors around that trailer immediately or you will be responsible for any accidents it may cause."

Rob and I went shopping for reflectors, but the two hardware stores we found would not take a credit card, and I hadn't carried much cash with me. A still small voice spoke to my spirit: *Walk around the block.* A sign in a store window announced those very reflectors on sale for *exactly* the amount of cash Rob and I had pooled together- nineteen whole dollars and eight cents. The Shepherd that promised to lead us had been there ahead of us, leveling our path.

After setting the warning signs around the boat, I went to town and called my dad. He felt so guilty when I told him what happened.

"It's all right, Dad," I said. "All's well that ends well." But it wasn't over yet.

"Mom, there's a motel pool with a slide. Can we stay there and wait for Dad?" Rob asked. I was happy to settle somewhere, have a nice dinner, and swim a while after all the trauma. To top it all off, God painted us a picture: a magnificent peachy gold sunset framed by craggy mountains reflecting in the glistening pool. What a way to end a supernatural day of deliverance from certain destruction.

In the meantime, after many phone calls, my husband Rog finally located an axle two hundred miles south of our Alpharetta, Georgia home. The unusual size axle we had to have was being tooled right then, and would be finished by the time someone arrived. What was the chance of that?

Our son Dave, who lived near us, offered to pick it up with his van. It took until two in the morning for him to get back to his dad. Dave turned the van and axle over to my husband, who took off in the night for Tennessee.

Not until he arrived in Lake City at six in the morning did Rog realize Dave hadn't given him the gas cap key. With great difficulty, he had to take apart the pipe leading to the gas tank to fill it.

I was jarred awake early by a knock on the motel door, but so thankful to lay groggy eyes on my weary husband. After a yummy breakfast we drove the few miles to the highway to check out the boat and trailer. It was gone, not a sign of it anywhere. I couldn't believe my eyes. I knew right where I'd left it, but Rog thought I was confused.

"How could anyone move it with a cracked axle and no tire?" he asked. We drove back to Lake City and asked a gas station attendant if he had seen a huge boat on the side of the road while driving to work. Just then a woman walking by 'happened' to overhear us, and said she had seen one being towed by a wrecker up the highway against traffic at 8 p.m. the evening before. She even 'happened' to know it was Brown's Wrecking Company in nearby Clinton, Tennessee.

She gave us directions, and we found it just where she had said. We learned from Mr. Brown the police had ordered him to haul the hazard off the highway, so he had taken it to his shop. It was a great relief to have a safe level parking area in which to repair the trailer. As owner of the lot, Mr. Brown charged us a fair towing fee, and even loaned us his tools. Any mechanic will attest that never happens.

While Rog tore the trailer apart to replace the axle, Mr. Brown directed me on my search for a bearing, a race, and two tires, since a second of the four had also been destroyed. The tires were a unique size, and not one was available within a fifty- mile radius. I stopped at a junkyard, my last hope, but to no avail.

    Sitting on a pile of tires to call places further away, I asked the Lord what to do. Just then the clerk yelled, "Wow! Can you believe this? Lady, you are sitting on the very tires you need!" He sold me two brand new tires for only ten dollars. I often pondered how rare sized new tires came to be in a junkyard.

    Following advice from every helpful clerk, I finally located a bearing and other items. I was disturbed on my return to find the bearing not in the bag. Rog examined the wheel and realized he hadn't needed one after all; I was relieved to find the parts store had also not charged me for it. That again confirmed God's invisible presence, and thrilled me to know He was so involved in every detail.

    Before sundown the new axle was in place, so Rog and Rob took off with the car and trailer. He had been unable to repair the trailer brakes, however, so I was very concerned about him driving through the mountains. "Please sleep in the boat overnight and fix them tomorrow," I pleaded.

He insisted they would be fine, and was determined to be home by midnight. At least the lug bolts were tight, but the trailer was no sturdier than before. Off they went, with me following in the van, praying fervently.

They climbed the first steep mountain, but on the descent the car started fishtailing as I watched in horror. They were soon out of control just as I had feared, heading for a steel rail; beyond was a huge chunk of nothing! I screamed for Jesus again, and in an instant, they stopped wobbling and straightened out as if nothing had happened. Rog said later he had told Rob, "Duck! We're going to crash!"

I turned into the next rest area, which Rog had passed up, turned off the engine and wept, still trembling. After a few moments, I turned on the key to catch up with them, but there was no response. I was flabbergasted. The battery was stone dead.

Eventually the entire rest area population took notice when I opened the hood, and surrounded me, trying to help. Nothing they tried worked.

Then I remembered God (yes, I admit I am not real swift!) and all the miracles I had just experienced, stood right in the midst of my new companions and humbly asked Him to start the van, slammed the hood shut, got back in, turned the key on, and away I flew, like Elijah in the chariot! My 'advisors' just stood there staring at my rear window. That would have been a perfect time for an altar call.

Soon I noticed my gas was nearly gone. "Lord," I prayed, as if He had no clue, "I have a problem here. I have no gas cap key and no cash. What do I do now?"

A voice somewhere inside said: *Follow that semi- truck ahead of you.* It immediately turned off at an exit, so I did too. There in front of me loomed a gas station, though there had been no sign of one, and no billboards. The attendant listened to my tale, reached in his pocket, and amazing me, opened my gas cap with his own key! He also accepted my MasterCard.

Entering our hometown, I stopped at a light, and there went the boat across my path at an intersection, heading safely home.

I have recorded only some of the many miracles God did on this trip. Whenever I am tempted to get discouraged, I remember what He has done for me in the past. The list is long and still growing. He promised to turn all things out for good for those that love Him, and He does.

Whether He guides us with thoughts, people, words, or inspirations, God can speak any way He wants. That's His business.

Supernatural is becoming the norm.

Jesus healed Rog of psoriasis when our prayer group prayed, leaving a small patch just to remind him. He healed him of bursitis as our prayer group prayed for him. His foot bone never really healed, but a circle of gristle holds it together, and he is free of the pain he had a long time.

When Rog went into the hospital with high blood sugars, he had a lot of pain in a hip, and was completely unable to walk. The nurse had to help him to the bathroom, and he was having an awful time. Nobody seemed to think that caused his problem, so they treated him for endocarditis, though no evidence appeared. They had taken Doplar sonograms and other tests, and all seemed in order.

In the meantime, the Sommers from church came and anointed him with oil and prayed for him, and within thirty minutes he was walking the halls, pain-free! His nurse was amazed, and so were we. She suspected he had been faking when she had walked him down the hall earlier!

About five years ago, Rog, who wore contacts for vision and an astigmatism, went forward in church because he was unable to drive at night due to broken blood vessels in his eyes. He asked for prayer for one eye that was much worse than the other.

Shortly after the prayer, he went for his regular check-up. The eye doctor took an entire afternoon, doing one test after another, and repeating some tests. Finally Rog asked him what was going on. The doctor admitted there was no possible mistake. He showed him the pictures with his name embedded right on it. The old picture showed several serious broken blood vessels which had led to blind spots all over his eye. The new picture showed that there was not one broken blood vessel, no blind spots, and on top of that, he now had perfect vision in that eye! He was so shocked, he did not know what to say.

So now Rog wears one contact (since he only asked prayer for one eye) and can again drive at night! This is a documented miracle. He gives God the credit. There is no earthly explanation.

2001 Hawaii, Here We Come!

The Holy Spirit inspired me with these words: "Prepare your heart to be my mouthpiece in Hawaii. I shall do whatever you allow me freedom to manifest for the purpose of setting captives free. Be prepared in your heart to share good news with those that will listen. I will fill your mouth with good things, and you will have this privilege if you will listen to my voice and obey me. I will confirm all with my word. I will not lead you astray, but will show you a clear path to follow. Obey Me. Keep your heart pure before me and I will show you my love. Go in peace."

October 19, 2001, shortly after America was forever altered by the attack of the Taliban, four of us caught the plane in Atlanta for Hawaii. Our friend Morey had lost his parents and needed a vacation. Our friend Arlene went as my roommate and Rog and Morey bunked together. We had no idea our cruise ship had gone bankrupt until we arrived at our hotel in Oahu, ready to leave the next morning.

  This is what happened. The towers of the World Trade Center collapsed on September 11, 2001, as a result of the center's Twin Towers being hit by jet airliners hijacked by terrorists affiliated with al Qaeda. Two of the four hijacked airliners crashed into the Twin Towers. The South Tower collapsed less than an hour after being hit by the hijacked airliner. Then the North tower went down. As a result, 2,752 people died, including all 157 passengers (including the hijackers) and crew aboard the two airplanes.

  Too weary to deal with it, we hit the sack. Before dawn, of course, we were wide awake due to the time difference. We had left home at 5 a.m. and flew in at 8 p.m. our time, which was 2 p.m. Oahu time. So we were up at 4 a.m. their time.

  Our travel agent arranged for us to fly to various islands, so we rented a van at each island. The first day we landed on Kauai, the garden island, and spent three days there. The next leg was flying to the big island, called Hawaii. There are two main towns here, Kona and Hilo, one at each end of the island with volcanoes in the center, one actively spewing molten lava!

After three days, from Kona we flew to Maui where we stayed seven days and flew to Los Angeles from there, nine hours of flying to get home.

So, let's back up to our arrival in Honolulu surrounded by flowers everywhere in and around the open airport. A girl met us, put real flower lei around our necks and kissed our cheeks, welcoming us to the islands! We found our rental van and drove to Waikiki Shores Hotel on the ocean.

By 7 p.m. we were settled and found Don Ho's restaurant with his live music. A clerk at Wyland gallery took my picture for me next to an awesome $28,000 painting. Rog and I got up early the next morning and walked to McDonald's for breakfast, followed by a swim in a huge pool. We were so happy.

We all took a boat out to a memorial in Pearl Harbor, which was bombed December

7, 1941 by the Japanese. We were standing above a sunken ship that still holds the dead sailors inside, walked the grounds of the memorial and read the remarkable history.

Two men in uniform, one American and one Japanese man confronted each other as I watched. Each one slowly raised his hand in salute to the other. I wept. It was an emotional scene after 9/11.

The next morning we left Waikiki beach, part of Honolulu on the island of Oahu and flew to Kauai (Kah Why' ee) and drove another van to the Radisson hotel on the shore of the azure Pacific in the town of Lihue. Chickens were cackling that early morning, and running all over the place...no crooked legged chickens there, I can tell you.

Monday morning Arlene found coconut syrup and we discovered guava jelly, and awesome corn chowder. Food was reasonably priced.

The last wonderful beach at the end of the road going east and north had a shallow coral reef. A tourist loaned me her mask and snorkel and I got to see some amazing sights! Two-foot long pipe or needlelike fish, a huge school of baby ones, butterfly fish, angelfish and a school of gray with yellow stripes about a foot long swam right past me!

Tuesday the Holy Spirit said, "My joy is your strength. Praise Me in and for everything. This is the way you reveal your trust in My sovereignty and how you break every fetter. You are in bondage if you cannot praise Me in all things. Take nothing for granted. Be thankful in every situation. I will pour rivers of living water into your innermost parts and joy will flow from you. Others will hunger for it. It is contagious, a strength in you that gives peace to others. Go in peace and joy!"

Yesterday. October 24 was fabulous! We went west from Lihue to the end of the road. The very end was blocked, but we saw the 'Grand Canyon' from the top of a mountain, about 4000 feet high, and ate quiche and fruit at the State Park up there. I saw my first round rainbow. It rains a bit every day.

Later from a dock a huge sea turtle swam beneath me! I recall the amazing story of five little Mexican fishermen lost at sea nine months. God answered their prayers, sent them over a hundred sea turtles and kept three of them alive all that time! (The other two could not keep the food in their stomachs and died.) They left Mexico and landed in Australia! It is recorded in the book, "The Fourth Fisherman" by Joe Kissack. Wow! Our God is so awesome!

We then found the old town of Hanapepe near the Green Garden Restaurant and I met an artist in her shop named Anna. She was a skinny little wrinkled woman with tattoos all over. Her eyes appeared to have cataracts, but it may have been spiritual stuff I was seeing. The eyes are the light of the soul, you know. Hers looked very strange, but she was a dear little person. She had very strange artwork. I asked if she liked to read, which she did, so I gave her my book and we exchanged Email addresses. She felt we were on the same plane – both spiritual. Well, we both deal with a spirit! I hope she finds mine. I claim her soul for the Lord Jesus.

October 24: Arrival in the city of Kona! The volcanoes are spewing on this island. At the airport, women were making gorgeous leis that smelled wonderful.

There are more Orientals than white people in Hawaii, Filipinos, Chinese, Japanese and Polynesians. We took our rental van to the King Kamehameha Hotel on the ocean. What a place! It had a mall below, pool, hot tub, marina and a vast cruise ship right outside.

Balmy breezes in the 80's caressed us as we walked into Bubba Gump's for breakfast. There are no bugs, so we ate next to the waves just outside the low wall. The waiter had a darling Jamaican Bubba imitation accent, and the food was spectacular.

Wal-Mart sold great inexpensive snorkels and masks with fins for only $30. What a deal. Rog and Arlene sat near a man weaving toys from rope or rattan in exchange for donations. I gave him a copy of my Scuba story, and he was thrilled. I am not sure he can read. Oh, well. While they watched, Morey and I swam at Kona's Lalal'ua Park. I almost bumped into a huge sea turtle; saw five in all; they have poor eyesight, and I saw wrasse, butterfly fish, gray fish and polka dot fish. It was so, so beautiful. Oh, what our wonderful Creator has made for us to enjoy! There is no end.

From there we found Volcano Park and a country restaurant. A fisherman carried in three large fish from his van, so I took a picture. One was a forty pound Mahi-Mahi and the others were Onos. He sold them for $3 a pound, live weight.

At the park we walked through a lava tube, a large tunnel made by molten lava leading to the ocean. We drove through a sulphur-smelling volcanic area that was still steaming! The size of the craters shocked us. One was at least a mile across. We stood at the edge and people below looked like ants. The visitor center showed a video of a live volcano. We declined a $225 ride in a helicopter to see the live volcano. I wish I had done it now.

The hotel mall exhibited the world record Marlin ever caught. It was 1062.5 pounds and fourteen feet six inches long-Pacific Blue Marlin, caught on a fifty-pound test line! Imagine that.

October 25: I studied Matthew 24 a while. A minister nearby was running a dive shop and saw my Bible, so we had an interesting visit about Jesus.

That day we visited Hilo on the other side of the island. A farmer's market had the best pineapple I ever tasted for $2. After supper we misread a woman's instructions on getting safely to Kona after dark. We ended up going home over the top of a mountain

6578 feet high at night. The one next to it was 11,863 feet high! It was a scary very bumpy ride for about two hours but we made it.

Saturday we flew to Maui and drove another van to the Aston Kannapali Shores condo on the glorious Pacific. Our suite was so beautiful, on the seventh floor overlooking the pool. We lunched at Pizza Hut and had supper at Denny's.

The King's Cathedral was a great treat for church. I bought a book there called, "I Was Married to Muhammed" by W. T. Call- quite an eye-opener! Pastor James Marocco had just returned from Dr. Cho's in Korea, the largest church in the world with over a million people! Can you imagine?

His message was excellent, about how hope precedes faith, being the action taken as a result of hope. We are chosen as the ones to hasten the return of Jesus by preaching the message. There are no lone rangers. We work together as one body. He shared about cell churches and how to avoid offenses.

The Lord gave me a dream. A man was turning from God, disappointed and in need of healing. God showed him he would be healed if he surrendered completely and let God have His way and seek only Jesus, not the healing. The man refused and was lost. Ouch. Good lesson.

We had lunch at Marco's with an Assemblies pastor and his wife from Illinois. God told Morey to buy their lunch. They were so grateful.

In the K-mart restroom a young woman was sobbing. She calmed down and told me her story. She was from Minnesota, was married ten years when she got cancer and was told she had a short time to live. Her marriage dissolved as a result. Then she found she had been misdiagnosed! She is fine and always dreamed of living in Hawaii. The cancer diagnosis had sped up her plans so she moved there. She came with an attorney to help him build up his business, using her skills with computers. He ended up filling up her credit cards. He deceived her by failing to tell her he had gone bankrupt. He took everything she had and abused her kindness by loading up her cards and not paying them off. She ended up sleeping in a tent on the beach!

Now she is living in her car, having cut off the arrangement. Her sister sent her a ticket to get home, but she has to leave her furniture and car behind, and was having a hard time with shame. She didn't ask for money; just needed to talk about it. She figured this was the end of the road and hope was gone. We had a good visit. We connected her with the church for help, and she realized God had sent us for her.

Monday we went north, saw a huge pineapple plantation and massive waves in the surf nearby. A rockslide on the road almost blocked our passage but we squeezed by. Everywhere are 'sacred stones' we are warned not to touch, just piled up rocks. We do not know what it means and nobody is able or willing to tell us. The road narrowed to one lane and we found Randy's Place, Panini Pua Kea, in the mountain wilderness, far from civilization. He raised star fruit, guavas, coconuts, three kinds of bananas, green oranges (they only turn orange with cold weather), passion fruit and mangoes, which were not in season. I gave him the book, *Does God Speak to Us?* He sprinkled rose petals on our heads. Cute. He loved having his picture taken with a front tooth missing and wearing his cowboy hat.

The Kaukini Gallery down the road was so beautiful. We missed the (closed) sculpture garden, the tropical gardens and a ranch...but our steps are ordered by the Lord.

Morey and Arlene got all gussied up for a Princess Dinner Cruise. They sat with newly wed Christians from Canada who work with the Salvation Army there. Arlene shared what she had learned about generational curses as God led her, and it was something they needed to understand. They had good prayer time together. Yes, God is in Hawaii, too.

While they were gone, Rog and I met the photographers selling photos of the cruise customers. She was a Full Gospel pastor's wife named Kristin Wood. She sells a picture of each couple with a folder holding a CD of the ship, cruise and the area, a frig magnet and a postcard for $20. Good idea. She bought my Motorcycle Miracle book for $5.

October 30-another wonderful day! Morey and Arlene got up at 4:30 a.m. for a snorkel trip to Molokini Island-the uninhabited crater. There were 54 snorkelers and several assistants to protect the swimmers and serve them. They were given noodles' and lifebelts and a helper in a kayak. We were proud of Arlene who doesn't swim, so this was quite a step of courage for her!

She saw wonderful sights for the first time. She came home all windblown but happy.

She is such a dear friend. This is a victory to love each other after being roomies for two weeks!

While they were gone, I took a scuba refresher course, but I didn't get to go out. One day I will. I have not used my scuba training in all these years.

The next day while the three of them napped on the beach, I was swimming and got pulled out to sea by a riptide, with only fins, mask and a snorkel. I asked Jesus to help me get back, while swimming furiously toward the shore and getting further out instead. I put my head under. The ocean floor was a long, long way down. My heart started racing. I was in trouble, and had never even heard of riptides. Gradually I realized I was also moving downstream and about two blocks away from Rog. "Lord, I am in trouble here! Please show me what to do!" Suddenly the current dissipated and I was able to swim to shore. Rog was oblivious to the pickle I was in, but he wouldn't have been able to help me out there. I won't swim alone any more!

On Front Street in LaHaina in Maui, we stopped to eat at Hecock's. God is so amazing. We had missed several Luaus, and here while we ate, a Luau was right outside our restaurant, over the little wall. It cost $100 a person including food, of course, but we got to see the whole show for the price of only our supper.

We headed for Keanae en route to Hana, only 55 miles but takes five hours due to the winding difficult roads, so we turned back. There is a farm here with 200 elk. Makowali is cowboy country.

November 1- Tom's birthday and time to go home! How difficult to leave paradise. I snorkeled a while, (never found one seashell!) left a book for my scuba instructor Mike about my three kids almost losing their lives in an underwater cave, and said goodbye to fat towels, great odors, the turquoise ocean, caressing winds, really special people...and coconut syrup!

We drove from Kannapali to LaHaina to the aquarium, and later ate crab cakes and bought shell necklaces, Hawaiian shirts at Kmart and followed the road going east through Kihei, Wailea to Makena. Breathtaking beauty! The beaches are all black and tan, covered with volcanic ash from up to 200 years ago.

The flight took all night to get home. Rog was blessed to get three seats in a row so he got to sleep all the way but we made it. Rob picked us up at the airport in his beautiful limousine and took us home in great style!

Leaping on...

January 4, 2003

Rog is a very sick man. New Year's eve, he started coughing. I moved onto the couch. At eight in the morning, I heard a huge crash and the house shook. I jumped up and ran to the bathroom. There was Rog, sprawled out on his face on the tile, just like 1997 when he had fallen down the stairs.

Awful memories came back. Either blood sugars or blood pressure or both made him fall. It was such a miracle nothing was broken. He did not have the strength even to lift his arms or legs. I gave him apple juice and dragged him to a softer carpet in the bedroom with his help, while he kept struggling to get up. His blood sugar was now up to 98. I took his pressure and it read 57/36- I called 911. Normal is 80-120 over 60-100. Dead is zero.

By then he was in a chair. He refused to go to the hospital. I gave him more juice. The EMT's arrived and got blood sugar readings of 30, 60, and finally 120-normal. They left, satisfied he was okay.

He went back to bed coughing. At noon, Rhonda brought over a thermometer, his temperature was 104, and his respirations were 40 a minute! Normal is 12-20. He was panting. Dr. Pastan said to get him to the hospital right away- the closest one. The ambulance returned and brought him to Cumming.

It is now evening. I am so tired, but cannot sleep, thinking about life and death and its implications. I know we are not going to be together all our lives, and one day we must part for a time. I cannot even bear the thought of such an event. God will help me, because I would never bear it alone.

His anemia is now critical, and red blood cells are necessary to carry much-needed oxygen, especially to his brain. How strange that this is the same place his dad was when we got married- needing transfusions.

It makes me wonder again about generational curses. What does it all mean? I am told Freemasonry is deceptive. Rog renounced his involvement years ago. His brother Ron has suffered beyond anything, his mom did, his dad did, and now him! I see Dave following in their footsteps with sickness and diabetes and all the stuff that goes with it. Yes, it is surely not from God. Jesus died to set us free from curses, but God said no curse comes without a cause. How can this one be broken? I have prayed every prayer I know, but it continues.

I play the what-if game. What if Rog left now? I am completely unprepared to handle life and finances. I would have no clue about money issues, paying bills, keeping up stock, paying taxes, fixing broken things, running the RV, or even the lawn mower!

I hope this is just a test to get me ready for some day far in the future. I am a jack-of-all-trades, but master of none. Whatever I do is imperfect, but I can do many things a little bit. I am still healthy and will have enough money to hire things done if I have to, and I would do that. But what kind of life would it be without Rog? I have no concept of being without him. We are a unit.

Others have made it, though it took time. God always got my friends through. In time, I would recover. All that matters in the end is that my faith remains, because we are only here for a visit, and nothing matters but eternity for me and Rog and all my family. I cannot complain. I have had a wonderful life, and I am part of God's kingdom, so I will never be alone. I can give my life for causes, for the kingdom of God, and for my family.

When the time comes for him to go on ahead of me, I will still have strength to encourage others, teach them, share my stories, and learn new skills. God will give me all the grace I need for whatever comes. He will never leave me nor forsake me.

I have taken Rog for granted so much. I appreciate him so much more. He has been such a faithful precious husband to me, and cared for me so well. He never complains about how he is feeling. His attitude is so good. It breaks my heart to see him in the hospital, all flushed and freezing, wrapped up in tons of covers and still cold, coughing and trying to breathe, having to get up all the time for the bathroom when he needs to just relax.

I can't stand watching them stick him, trying to find a good vein all the time, and waking him up for vital signs just when he finally gets to sleep. However, I understand.

Life is just not about us. It is all about Jesus. Either we are born again, and He has taken residence in us, or we are not, and He has not. If He has, we are part of each other, and will never really die. When we get to heaven, we will see that relationships with others are part of that oneness. I see why Jesus calls us the body of Christ.

I am so thankful for dear precious children, daughter-in-laws, grandkids, friends and cousins, and my wonderful Mom, Dad, and step dad, already in heaven, and my awesome family in Michigan. How can I think I would not make it through if Rog passed ahead of me? Of course, it would be the biggest crisis in my life, but it too would pass, and life would go on. God is good, and His mercy endures forever. His plans for us are for good and not for evil. If God is for us, who can be against us? God is Love.

Lord Jesus, come quickly! I love you.

August 6, 2003

We are so blessed. I took a shower, and it felt so wonderful. I am so grateful for nice hot, pure, plentiful water. I thank God for giving us water. It is probably our most valuable resource. Well, then I think of clean air, free of pollution, clear and easy to breathe. Surely this is the most important resource we have. Water is second. But we need them both.

Then I think of food, which we can't live without. We have access to all the foods of the entire world right in our stores. We have money to buy them, stoves to cook on, cold storage to preserve them, and families to enjoy them. We are so, so blessed.

I sensed the Holy Spirit speaking this to me this morning. "Daughter, I have a word for you. Peace. This is a gift for you today. My peace I give you, not as the world gives. I give it to you.

Nobody else can give you this gift. It has to come from me. I am the Prince of peace. I bestow good gifts upon those I love, just as you desire to do for those you love.

When the world closes in on you, sit back and call on me, and this peace will rest on you again, as you contemplate my ways and my power and my love for you.

January 6, 2004

Yes, this is a repeat performance of last year!

Rog got dizzy and crashed to the tile floor Friday morning, 1/2/04. His blood sugar and his blood pressure were low and he could not sit up. He recovered after juice, but came down with a fever. Dr. Pastan's nurse told us to go immediately to the closest hospital so we went to Cumming. He has bacterial pneumonia, and is recovering from that.

The problem now is that he has had two pints of blood for critical anemia, and the source of anemia is not found. Loss of blood, destruction of blood cells or not creating new cells may have brought his anemia suddenly to 26. No wonder he can't even think straight sometimes. It is a mystery. Recent changes to examine have been pneumonia, antibiotics, Tylenol, (prescribed but not allowed with Coumadin) a different insulin, (Humalog) and/or missing three doses of Creon last week. His protein intake is down to three ounces a day due to proteinuria. Could he have a bleeding ulcer in his stomach? No evidence. He has frequent stomach pain, but not related to food in timing. Doc assumed it was his pancreatitis flaring up.

We just learned that beta blockers mask symptoms of hypoglycemia, so he was unaware of a blood sugar drop until he finally took a test. He has been very low in the mornings; 47 or so, and has cut down his insulin to 2 units a day. Normal blood sugars for him are 80 to 140.

If it is a B12 deficiency, would the lack of protein contribute? If so, would B12 shots make up for the lack? Shouldn't he stay on vitamins and minerals in the hospital? They cut all those things. What other tests can be taken? Should he have a Guaiac test? It shows blood in the stool. Coumadin is a greater risk if one has intestinal problems. Could it be the chronic pancreatitis?

The doctor on staff here said we need one strong medical coordinator for Roger's medications who will monitor them all and determine what not to take. He seems concerned about drug interactions and side effects. Could this be causing the anemia? Nobody dares admit such things.

I learned a lot. I read that trauma within vessels caused by artificial heart valves damages red blood cells, and abnormal RBC's have a short life span. Caffeine ingested while on Coumadin increases bleeding. Nobody told us that. Vitamin K deficiency increases the risk of bleeding! Where does he get it? He is not allowed green leafies on Coumadin. Vitamin K is required for the production of clotting factors. The body has very limited ability to store the vitamin. Yikes!

The good old Internet has us thinking, but we still need to understand the cause of anemia.

April 11, 2004 Rog got healed.

Last Wednesday for no good reason Rog threw up. He hardly ever throws up, no matter how sick. Then he was fine. Friday he had pain in his lower abdomen. By Sunday morning he also had a low grade fever, weakness, and was dizzy. I called the doctor, since we had nearly lost him only a month ago with a bleeding ulcer. His BP was 149/47 lying down. The doctor said to go to emergency if his BP was lower standing than lying down. It was 115/49. An hour later, after I showered and loaded the car for the hospital, it was 113/47. By the time I got ready to go, it was down to 95/35!

By then, I had called Pastor Kelly at church. I was so glad he had answered the phone. I knew the church would be praying. I had done and said all I knew to do all night. I didn't want to give in, but God uses doctors, too. I was by then convinced the ulcer must not have been gone, and was flaring up. I took one more BP reading before leaving. It was 135/52!

God answered again! He gave us another miracle. I am so relieved. Maybe the enemy attacked just to test us and get us scared. If we took his offer, we could have gone through all that awful stuff again! Praise the Lord! Jesus reminded me that even when he prayed, often it happened 'within the hour.' Sometimes if it is not immediately evident, we give up and figure God said no. Not true!

I just realized the promises I stand on for my own salvation are the same as those I stand on for my family, especially Tom. If I expect them to work for me, will they work for them? Yes, they will work for all of us. It is crucial that I continue to stand firm in my faith on all of God's promises. Without them, I have nothing. Feelings are not valid evidence of hope for my future, and even experiences can be misunderstood. Only God's word can be trusted. If it is not true, none of the rest even matters!

We are camping in the RV in Fort Myers. Rog was getting so weak, but claimed he never saw any evidence of losing blood. He got terribly weak, and stayed at the hospital eight days with a bleeding intestinal ulcer, and had several pints of blood. It was only by God's miracles he did not leave us, having lost 2/3 of his blood! He is better every day, but is always cold. God has been SO good, repairing and healing.

The other night Rog got a 103 fever, and the Lord healed him in an hour. The Sunday before, Rog was attacked by low blood pressure of 69/39! God healed that too, and we went on to church. It happened every Sunday morning for three weeks. But we are praying ahead now!

Journal May 5, 2004

Does stress affect our bodies? My dear husband is again in the hospital! He had pneumonia for a week the first of the year, and conquered that, except for a strange anemia that was not solved. Occult stool tests were done, but no blood loss showed up. He rests a lot, and his energy level has not been normal for his age.

Two weeks ago, Rog fell backwards trying to get his leg over his bicycle, and hit his head on the sandy ground here in Fort Myers. His neck was a bit sore, and he was dizzy for about an hour, and walked the bike home. We debated about getting a checkup but he felt he would be fine shortly. He perked up, but the next day he woke up dizzy and weak as a cat. (Are cats necessarily weak?) We tried to figure out all the options. His sugars were normal, but his BP was very low- 86/37. We took it three times, and by the third it was normal. By afternoon, he was doing all right, and we had friends in for supper who were leaving the next day.

The next morning, he was weak and sort of pale and tired looking. We had called the doctor before and visited with the pharmacist about medications and possibilities. His PA (physician's assistant) in Atlanta said it could be low salt, since he was on salt restriction. We gave him a banana in case his potassium was low, and a little salt. He perked up a bit, but not as much as the day before.

By the third day, Rog we definitely in trouble of some sort. He was eating breakfast, and his hands were trembling slightly. His hands were ice-cold, and his fingernails did not fill with blood when pressed. I knew he was in big trouble. He finally agreed maybe we needed to take some action, where the day before he didn't think it was necessary. He had shown me a stool sample, and it sure looked reddish to me around the edges. He had been on iron until a short time before this, so blood would not have shown. Iron turns stools real dark.

I asked the PA in Atlanta on the phone about it, and he doubted if it was really blood, because he said blood would have been dark or black or like coffee grounds. But he had no idea why the stool was red. (Fresh blood maybe?) The new medication for a yeast infection on Rog's mouth would not turn it that color, he said. We decided to go to emergency right away.

I got cleaned up, and his brother Ron was sitting with him. Suddenly Rog's eyes went white and he passed out for a moment. Ron didn't tell me then what he saw for some reason, but came and whispered, "Get him to the hospital fast!"

By then, he was having trouble getting down the steps! I knew then we made a mistake by not calling an ambulance, but it was too late. We got him into the car with great difficulty, and I took him to Lee Memorial, which has a great reputation for cardiac patients.

Ron and Bev came soon afterwards in his truck, and only then did he finally tell me Rog had passed out! Tests were done on him right away once we got him into triage and admitted. His hematocrit was four! Normal is 12-17 or so, meaning he had no red cells left to carry oxygen to his body! The doctor said he would probably not have lived another day as he had lost 2/3 of his blood somewhere!! It is still not known today where the bleeding is coming from. His Coumadin level was sixteen! Normal for him was 3.5 or less.

That meant his blood was thin as water! He was given four pints of blood that first day alone, in addition to magnesium sulfate and fluids. He also had a chest x-ray, and a cat scan, probably to make sure his brain was not bleeding from his fall. They were probably trying to figure out why he was still alive! Only God.

The doctor checked his stomach in the afternoon and found a large mass about his pubic bone, and wondered if there was a problem there. A Foley catheter was put in, and the mass was urine- about 450 ml! The bladder can hold 500 ml.

By evening, he no longer looked like a pale ghost, but looked human again! I went for supper, and came back to find him violently shaking the whole bed with chills. He now had a fever of 101.3. He was given IV antibiotics called Rocephin.

Jumping a few years...

October 9, 2009 from the Holy Spirit

"Be still and know that I am God. I will speak when you are quiet and expectant to hear my voice. You have many questions and you are concerned about so many things. I am meek and lowly of heart. I am he that takes your burdens and gives you a light burden to carry. I will take your yoke upon me and carry those things that weight you so heavily, and you will float like a balloon filled with helium.

I am the one you called upon many years ago, and you surrendered your life to me. You have taken it back may times and gone your own way, thinking you were following me. You were leading...but I was not behind you.

Come to me, all that are labored and heavily laden and I will give you rest. My ways are not as your ways. My ways are higher than yours. I am doing things in your family you cannot see. You are a light shining in the darkness, but you cannot see that you are that light. Let your light so shine that the path is easy for those who come after you to follow. They are seeking the path. They need a clear path. Make it easy to follow. They cannot find it if the way is obscured by weeds and slippery stones. It must be level and clear of debris. Debris is sometimes guilt, shame, or even grief. These things clutter the path and cause one to turn back in discouragement.

The days are difficult for many. Remember when I told you I will shake all that can be shaken so what is on a sound foundation will stand. These are the days of shaking. Those that have built their house upon the rock will not fall. They may see through a glass darkly and confusion may rule in their hearts, but when the dust has settled they will see the rock on which they stand. The unimportant things will fade away and what is made of gold will shine brightly. Go in peace."

November 3, 2009

Rog gets a heart cath tomorrow in spite of the risk to his kidneys. They feel giving Mucomist and sodium bicarbonate will protect them. I pray they are right. His cardiac enzymes were up and he had a heart attack in January. They want to see if his mitral valve is causing congestive heart failure and the need for oxygen. It was probably just the result of Rog thinking he was dehydrated and drinking lots of fluids, and then taking Torsemide, a diuretic. But then he quit before getting rid of all the excess fluid and it built up around his heart and lungs, bringing him to the hospital for oxygen to breathe. It was just in time! Next day would have been too late. He would have suffocated at home. He was gasping for breath.

Now the docs want to see in there, but the risk to his kidneys seems too great to me. If they find a damaged mitral valve---then what? He can't take another operation! The dear man has gone through so much and never complains! He just loves hospital food. I do not know how they can cook so well unless he is getting stuff not on my list!

November 4, 2009

Rog spends his birthday in the hospital.

I must go to bed- I am numb. Rog would likely have suffocated here at home last Saturday if we had not gone to emergency Friday. After sitting in there a few hours on oxygen with congestive heart failure and lots of fluid around his heart, he suddenly got to where he could not breathe! Thank God they moved fast and hitched up a ventilator and literally saved his life.

Today, in spite of grave danger to his already damaged kidneys, the doctors had to use a dye to do a heart catheterization, going through the femoral artery in the groin all the way through the heart. They suspected a damaged mitral valve, but the doctor said it was fine. They did find he was a heart attack just waiting to happen. One large artery was 95% blocked so he got a stent- and is doing wonderfully.

We prayed and believed God heard our prayers of faith (otherwise no sense wasting time praying-ha) and is protecting his kidneys. The doctors are closely monitoring him for the next couple days. We are thrilled with his new energy. He is off oxygen as of 2 p.m. and walking already. The repair should help his kidneys do much better as well.

Hallelujah! God is so good. He gave us wonderful doctors and guided their hands.

Today the heart doctor told Rog he does need a mitral heart valve! They only examined one side of his heart for some reason. It looks like the blockage was leading to the mechanical valve.

When I arrived, Rog told me the doctor said perhaps the valve will 'settle down' or something- it gave him hope that he may not need surgery.

Dr. Pastan said to expect the best results. We are. His urine looks good to me. I wonder if they are not giving much Lasix in case the kidneys cannot take the stress just yet. He is still on oxygen because of the fluid load around his lungs. He feels bloated and his legs and feet look fat, but they are not making prints. "God will perfect what concerns us. Nothing shall by any means harm us."

November 9, 2009 Standing Vigil... Still in the hospital.

Rog is slowly improving. His blood loss seems to be decreasing. His kidneys show improvement as the creatinine level goes down. I believe his kidneys will be all right, as long as no surgery is needed on his heart.

The doctor numbed his throat with yukky stuff and put a scope down his esophagus. He did an echocardiogram from that area onto his mitral valve without the need to use any more dye. We are waiting to learn the results. If the valve is prolapsed or turned inside out, the doctor said he may be a candidate for a procedure called clipping rather than doing surgery. It can be done through the femoral artery in his groin.

This afternoon I stood guard outside the door of his hospital room to keep everyone out so he could sleep for a change. He gets wakened all night long. He must be exhausted. He got three hours in this afternoon.

November 11, 2009

Two nights ago Rog woke up feeling sticky. His IV had jammed and he was lying in a pool of blood. Funny the doctors never consider that blood loss part of the problem! They say it is heart valve leakage, intestinal leakage, but never the result of accidents or even the numerous blood tests they take every single day!

Last night it happened again, just after he got a pint of blood. What a waste of that precious life-giving substance. Then the nurse took his vital signs and found something was wrong, so she tried to wake him. She took his blood sugar and it was forty! So he got a snack and IV sugar. What a war this is!

This morning the heart doctor came in while we were on the phone, so I got to hear a bit of it. He said he wants Rog on Plavix and aspirin for a month at least and hopefully for three months. Rog told him he cannot tolerate it because of bleeding but the man insisted. He also told Rog he may still do something with his heart valve! Rog had told me it was minor and they were not doing anything- he got that from the nurse, I found. Nothing is making sense to me lately.

We will see if Dr. Pastan lets Rog go home to continue the kidney recovery or not. The blood loss, we are told, will continue until Rog is off those meds. The Piedmont Hospital heart doctor confuses me.

December 18, 2009

Why do we decide to trust in God? Does He look around for someone to give a gift of faith to? Do we hear the message and make a logical decision based on the facts and choose Him? Are we in an emotional state that presses upon us a need for Him?

There are millions of reasons people choose to believe in and follow God. He has unique ways of wooing each of us to Him at some point in our lives. I have heard of some that hear of Him for the first time, and accept Him. Others are a lot tougher, exposed over and over to the gospel, and do not give in to Him until they are up against a brick wall they cannot scale. The Bible says the Holy Spirit reveals Him to us.

My husband is up against that brick wall. His leaky heart valves are causing constant blood loss. Recently he got a transfusion and it caused a heart attack. His kidneys, already damaged by diabetes after forty years, cannot handle more surgeries on his body. They will shut down if the doctors repair his heart, and his life will be spent in the dialysis clinic. He chooses not to have surgery, but to trust God to keep him going and heal his heart.

He has been given many miracles over the years and knows God has the power and the will to heal him. He is prepared to pass on if it is his time to go to heaven and has his ticket. The Bible says, "Believe on the Lord Jesus Christ and you shall be saved." He does.

Our pastor anointed him with oil according to the command in James 5, and prayed the prayer of faith. Our friends and family have asked God to heal him. We know God cannot lie. It is impossible for God to lie. That means we can trust what He says. He says He is our Great Physician and heals all our diseases. He said He sends His Word and heals us. He said life and death is in the power of the tongue and we will eat the fruit of it.

Jesus came to earth to show us the Father, and what did He do? He healed all that came to Him. He is still alive and intercedes for us. His power has not diminished. Psalm 103:3 says He heals all our diseases. I Peter 2:24 says by His stripes we were healed. Only one problem. We must believe it with a whole heart and confess it no matter what others may think of us.

Some friends think I talk like I believe God because I am afraid to admit he could die. I am well aware he could die. I am prepared for that possibility- but until that time I will continue to trust God. If this is his time to go, he will go with my faith still intact. I do not fear death, for myself or for him. We know our God is faithful, and His grace is sufficient.

December 26, 2009

The other day I was raking and burning leaves when my ankle started hurting. Before long the other one hurt, and soon I was hobbling around, unable to bend either one. The pain was getting unbearable, and I sat down watching the fire thinking, "What is happening to me all of a sudden?"

Every day when I get up a verse pops in my head. That day it was, "The enemy comes to steal, kill and destroy. I have come (Jesus said) that you may have life, and that more abundantly."

'Leaning unto my own understanding', I decided I better call the doctor and get my ankles checked out for arthritis. Then I realized he could only give me medicine in hopes of relieving pain. He couldn't heal it. Is it possible Satan sent the pain? I recalled another verse. "Submit yourselves to God; resist the enemy and he must flee."

I offered myself to the Lord 'as a living sacrifice' and commanded the spirit of infirmity to leave me in Jesus' name. Nothing happened. I tried again. Still nothing. For the next hour I spoke God's promises aloud and continued to tell spirits to leave me alone, spirits of arthritis, a spirit of pain, and Satan as well. The pain just got worse. I kept thanking God for healing me and went back to raking. A few minutes elapsed before I realized the pain had left me completely.

It could have been something explainable, or it could have been an attack from the thief. I cannot prove what it was, but I learned something. We are often too quick to grab medication before we seek God for the answer. Then we have to deal with the side effects, which are sometimes worse than the original problem.

Stop the Medicines

We have a friend who got arthritis. Before long he was in a wheelchair almost incapacitated. He was given powerful medications, but only got worse. Finally he was on chemotherapy and morphine as well as another powerful drug, and was nearly frozen in place with pain. He and his wife prayed daily and even had communion together every morning for over a year after he got sick.

One day he got sick and threw up for three days straight. His medicine would not stay in his stomach. On the third day, he realized his pain was all gone! He was completely well, able to walk and move with no discomfort. He didn't sleep for a few nights because his body was withdrawing from the morphine, but he was so thrilled to be free of pain, that was only a minor inconvenience for him. Today he is still well and happy.

Did God make him sick to get the medicine out of him? Maybe He did. He seemed to be showing him he didn't need it because he was no longer sick. Was it a miracle? Yes, God surely answered his prayer and healed him.

My husband has been diabetic over forty years. It has taken its toll on his poor body, despite his diligent obedience to all the doctor's orders. We have been reading many promises in the Bible about healing, and our faith is growing steadily as we become convinced God wants us well.

How do we conquer thinking patterns ingrained nearly since birth? Most of them are incorrect for members of God's kingdom. Once we enter this realm, we are no longer subject to the natural laws that dominated us all our lives. We must begin to think like God thinks. If we can agree with God, put Him first, worship Him and trust Him, anything is possible for us. He said it, and He cannot lie.

The doctor said to get his life in order and stay as peaceful as he could until his time came. We asked what he thought about us going to Florida in our RV for the winter.

"Sure", he said. "Why not? They have doctors there to give him blood and suck the fluid out of him." We got excited about going. We have many friends with great faith at the campground, and a wonderful church. Bill Bazansky has a great Bible study and this man has great teaching and much faith for healing.

I was getting convinced that God would heal him, and got excited when I realized there was a lot of hope in God's Word. Maybe I didn't have to lose him after all. God was able to do anything. When friends asked how he was doing, I said, "He will be just fine. God is healing him, and he will overcome this. Without a test there is no testimony."

It all sounded good, and I was not about to be 'double-minded' and waver in my faith, but when my son, a man of faith, a man I trust, sat me down and forced me to be 'realistic,' I looked with my five senses and buckled. What a fool I had been. I was simply living in denial. He is dying. What if he dies in Florida and I am all alone with a motor home to get home, and a body to get back to Atlanta? What was I thinking? What if I drove it and someone was killed because I had an accident?

He has gone from 175 pounds down to 140, and is white as a sheet. The doctor said he has a leaky heart valve, congestive heart failure, fluid on his lungs and heart, and then they found almost all his arteries are nearly closed leading to his heart. He will need weekly transfusions, but when he got one recently, it caused a heart attack, his second. He can barely walk to the kitchen for lunch.

Tossing and turning, trying to sleep, peace eluded me. I was so positive, and so able to handle life when there was hope. Denial, is it? Or is this hope based on truth? Denial has no foundation. It is an illusion based on lies. No, this hope is different. It is based on

God's commands to us. 'Transform your mind into the mind of Christ.' We must stop thinking as the world thinks. 'Man cannot live by bread alone, but by every word that proceeds from the mouth of God.' Yes, there is a battle of the mind to be fought, but there is a victory around the corner. How do other people win their miracles? They do not come by accident. They come after we travail in prayer, search for God with all our hearts, petition Him, believe His promises without wavering, and we receive what He offered.

Most people today do not travail in the spirit. We fight little skirmishes with the enemy, but he keeps coming back. We stand a while, but then we climb back into the world and forget who and whose we are. We need to learn to stand until the battle is over and we have won. Missionaries pray and fast sometimes for days, worshiping God, and coming into the Holy of Holies, purified, repentant, and clean before Him, covered with His righteousness, cleansed by His blood. Many come into agreement, and they all believe alike, confessing the Word over the sick one until he is set free. They never leave until the battle has ended. We know nothing of such commitment.

I decided whether we wait for the miracle to manifest before we leave, or we go expecting it, we will live in peace and not in fear. Our son was attacked the same way we were, with fear, and we caught it too. Faith and fear cannot exist together.

We choose life and blessing. We will not judge by what we see with our eyes. We will not listen to critics. They only prove the devil is worried. We will pray over medicines we take and ask God to protect us from side effects or ask Him to show us if we should take them at all.

January 2, 2010

What a day. Our Minnesota friends Carol and Lonnie were staying with us on the way to Florida. We had a nice quiet New Year's Eve and went to bed early. 12:30 AM Rog sat up feeling weird. I listened to his heart and it was skipping beats. No pain. Breathing 32 times a minute. (Normal is 12 to 20 at most) BP OK. Mouth tingling. Trouble breathing a bit. Tried to check blood sugar- couldn't get enough blood.

Called his doc and got a message. Called 911, and the EMT mentioned nitroglycerin. I gave him a nitro tablet. He still felt clammy and weak, and his eyes went back in his head a moment. 911 headed out. I unlocked the door and Carol woke up, guiding in five guys. They did an EKG, got him walking-or tried- and he wobbled to the gurney. In the ambulance they got an IV going.

Tests were done in ER- Cumming. Waited for results from 1 AM until almost 5 when they finally started fluids ` for dehydration and gave him 4 baby aspirins and an IV with glucose. The doc thought he might have had another heart attack because his heart enzymes were up but Dr. Williams said not for sure. He woke up. I went home at 5:30.

He had decided on his own to take two Torsemide (diuretics) that morning- too many to pump out only one pound of fluid. Also had a UTI (urinary tract infection) we found today. Good thing we went in. He now has Dr. Hershey from Johns Creek Emory, and Dr. Hermoni- a friend of Dr. Williams, working through Cumming. We are in good hands. Rog seems at peace, relieved at getting good care. He can relax and let them give him insulin and pills without thinking what to do next. An echogram showed the area of damage-lower left ventricle. Fluid accumulates around his lungs and he has trouble without oxygen. He was taken off beta blockers because they hurt his kidneys.

Bottom line is he needs two new valves and several opened arteries, but would destroy his kidneys, so it is not practical and will surely not improve his quality of life. A pacemaker may help the skipped beats, diuretics can help PRN (as needed) and oxygen can ease the burden on his heart.

January 4, 2010

Rog is off oxygen- praise God! He got a pint of blood. Dr. Pastan called to check on him to admit him if he was not in the hospital. My questions were about the clip procedure, how many the doctors have done, and why is he still on Plavix (a second blood thinner) if the stent is closed up? These are the things that take lives. Doctors have to weigh greater and lesser evils sometimes. They are not God but they do the best they can. We are so blessed with good doctors.

An evangelist friend of ours, Kim Klaudt, was wonderful Sunday night in Austell! He preached about how God talks to us…in our spirit.

I brought my grandson Mitch and his wife checks for Christmas, and he gave me a picture that said they gave a gift to the hungry this year. He makes me proud to be his grandma. He may have a child someday. They fell in love with their nephew Daniel.

January 13, 2010

Interesting day. Dropped Rog off at the doctor's office and parked. The doc simply said heart surgery is our only option, and there is a tiny chance the kidneys would survive, but he could give no odds. We would have to be prepared for dialysis. He told a bit about dialysis, and some about kidney transplants, not really an option, and big major surgery, with permanent immune drugs, and fluid buildup.

We learned the heart attack was moderate. He has not lost blood since last week. Great news. All labs were fairly good. His oxygen level is 98%. He still has fluid in both lungs and needs the diuretic probably every two of three days from now on. The bare metal stent done by Piedmont has already closed up. The doc knew 50% do close up but he had few options! He must stay on nasty blood thinner Plavix and aspirin anyhow because other arteries are also almost closed! Yuck. Potential for more bleeding.

Why is he so exhausted? Gets up a lot to get rid of fluid, hard to breathe lying down; may need oxygen at night but it is not covered by Medicare. I wonder why! He will get it anyhow, of course.

Kara, the nurse, said even a marathon runner who lies in bed two days takes a month to fully recover all his strength! Seven days is that much worse. Rog must exercise daily, starting even walking five minutes and working his way up. Impossible, it seems to me.

January 18, 2010 Spiritual warfare

God is showing me I must seek out sword scriptures for my situation the same way a soldier carefully chooses his weapons for different situations. I must saturate my mind with the Word and put it first, before cleaning house or any other thing. It is most important. Pray, anoint, speak, and worship God. Agree verbally with God, alone and with others. Fasting can't hurt, either.

What am I feeling? In the night I get attacked by spirits that lie to me. They tell me I will be alone and lose my faith because God will not give me what I want.

My answer is like Job. Though he slay me or Rog, I will serve Him. His will be done, not mine. I know His will from the Word. If I have misunderstood it, He will explain it to me when I need it. My prayers can save my husband just like the women in Hebrews.

"My son, despise not thou the chastening of the Lord, nor faint when thou art rebuked of him."

I need words to tell others when they ask how things are going. God reminds me that by my words I am justified or condemned. Life and death are in the power of the tongue. There is no testimony without a test. Raise up the standard of Christ's blood and the word of our testimony to overcome, and also love not our lives unto death.

January 26, 2010 Respiratory distress

Rog landed back in ICU with respiratory distress. This is what happened. I am becoming very cautious about the procedures! A nurse took Rog (in his bed) late in the night (when he was already exhausted from tests) for a nuclear scan to check his lung fluid, and did it all alone. That must be when the machines are available...no matter a person desperately needs rest.

She laid him down flat while his lungs were fluid filled. He tried to get her attention but she was deaf! He started drowning and stopped breathing! Thank God a nurse came along (who later told us what had happened). She found him blue and not breathing. She quickly clamped a biPAP machine on his face!

After the nurse went her way, the deaf one continued lying him down to complete her task while he struggled! That is sadistic! The machine on his face was so tight he couldn't stand it. (He still had marks on his face several hours later.) He said later that she continued the procedure for about two hours while he laid flat! It never should have happened to begin with. He was not in distress until she messed with him.

His doctor must have found out because he asked Rog a lot of questions, and then put him through more tests (with no food again, of course) to prove he had not suffered a stroke, heart attack, or pulmonary embolism.

The tests kept him there two extra days and two more days of skipping meals. He is so unbelievably thin! I am getting scared of hospitals- even when they appear to be making him well. He is better after two days home than he ever was there! He can rest and eat. The only thing they did to help him was give him a pint of blood- which he needed because a doctor put a stent in his heart artery and said he had to keep it clear with Plavix and Aspirin- on top of Coumadin! Three blood thinners.

Later...

This morning I found him in ICU again. He was put on Heparin-another blood thinner- so now we really have to pray against blood loss. The doctor decided if he has had a pulmonary embolism or a heart attack he would need blood thinner. They also plan to do a scope on his heart valve to see if he had a blood clot. He was just overloaded with fluid.

He is so weary, but nobody ever lets him sleep more than fifteen minutes. We pray he will stabilize and get out of there and there will be no bleeding from any orifice. We pray his heart works better and the fluid leaves the wrong places. We pray the diuretic does not do any more kidney damage, and he can get some rest and be able to eat enough to stay alive. He is not eating hardly anything because the fluid presses against his abdomen.

Last evening a nurse came in to rinse his central IV line with heparin. I said I didn't think he was supposed to have that. She checked and came back with a big sign over his bed- NO HEPARIN! Guess I was right.

He does not want me to leave him, but I went home for a bit to check messages and rest. I put my key in the lock, and the inside of the lock fell on the ground! I couldn't get into my own house. Rob came over and took a hammer to it and I got in. The roof vent for the plumbing is leaking and when it rains, it fills a bucket in the attic. My check engine light had gone off but has come back on!

Let's see….what else? Rob got the flu and is well. Now Chandler has it!

God intervened: Rog's hemoglobin went up two points again even though he was given no more blood! 9.7 to 11.2. That is the second time that happened. Encouraging. It means he was not bleeding for a couple days or God transfused him! We prayed his oxygen level would rise and it went from 89% on oxygen to 100% in five minutes! He is recovering from a urinary tract infection. He lost his hearing and scared me so. Vancomycin can cause hearing loss. His hearing is back. (I forgot why he was on it.) He has Christian nurses that are so kind. He was thrilled to find his doctor is from Israel- such a compassionate man, Dr. Hermoni, who holds his hand while he talks to him.

My friend came to the hospital with me and we played a game about being thankful, going around and taking turns telling what we are thankful for. Rog still has gratitude, and his attitude is not totally negative, which amazes me!

February 2, 2010

I am reading a shocking book called, "Confessions of a Medical Heretic" by Dr. Mendelsohn- a prominent doctor. He said, like I watched happen to Rog, people can starve while they do tests, colonoscopies, stomach scopes, and try to keep intestines empty so he won't bleed.... while what they gave him caused the bleeding in the first place!

True. Rog had no food or water for three days and had no IV giving him fluids! I complained continually about it, but they just said it had to be. I was so worried about him surviving! They seemed to have no concern for this but it is so necessary. The book tells how pharmaceuticals are not what we think. So often the medication side effects are the same as the disorder they are given to cure. He calls the medical profession a religion and indeed it is. We are required to trust our doctor with our life. Only Jesus can be trusted. God said the man is cursed who puts his trust in man! Most of us humans have wrong motives. The love of money is the root of all evil. Nobody is immune to its temptations.

How shocked we were when our other heart doctor told us the stent from November was already blocked by December! It did no good at all, and the surgery took a toll with stress, destroyed more of his kidneys and did much harm. He lost half his blood again because of the three blood thinners. He could have died or had another heart attack like he did in November. While he was having a transfusion, his heart got overloaded, causing the attack.

He was rushed to Piedmont hospital where the stent seemed to be a solution. The doctor considered a clip procedure on a mitral valve which the heart attack damaged. The heart had enlarged in an attempt to pump blood through the body. An enlarged heart spreads out so heart valves won't shut tightly. The heart can't pump blood through the body effectively.

The doctor admitted that his kidneys would not survive the surgery, so he would live on dialysis the rest of his short life! Rog refused the surgery.

We will be challenged by excess fluid or blood loss to return to the hospital and Rog asked me to agree to keep him home. His veins are now so damaged by puncturing them so often they cannot get blood. He will again require a central line leading right to his heart by stitching the line into his neck.

What happened since November? How can we avoid it next time?

This is a recent record of Roger Parrott's medical history. I record it to uncover a pattern so perhaps we can learn how to break this family curse. Why do some get so sick and others stay so healthy?

Tonsillectomy and circumcision age 7

Adult onset diabetes from age 27

Cyst and tailbone removed 1959

Retinopathy, cataract surgery both eyes, vitreous humor removed from left eye

Bladder neuropathy-intermittent catheter used daily many years

Anemia

Bacterial Endocarditis 1995

Mechanical aortic valve and two bypasses 1997

Chronic pancreatitis from 1999

Intestinal artery stent 2007

Cardiac stent 11/2009

Pneumonia 2007, 2009

Mild heart attack January 2009 and 11/09

Ulcerative colitis or Crones or IBS, intestinal ulcers and stomach ulcers-healed.

Leaky mitral valve

Kidney failure

March 8, 2010 Hospital

Dear Lord,
    You answered my prayer again. Thank you. I asked you to give me a sign about getting Rog to the hospital or allowing him to have his way and die tomorrow at home. I could not comply with his wishes. Where there is life, there is hope. I sounded real brave to let him stay home and ignore the signs of impending death, but when it comes down to it, I cannot accept that responsibility, especially when he is not totally cognizant of even his surroundings at the moment.
    So you sent Priscilla, our dear home health nurse, to evaluate him. Just at the right time, his blood pressure chose to take a

nosedive, first from what I had taken earlier, 117/54. It went to 98/48- very low, in a few minutes, to 88/42! There was our first sign.

Then Priscilla asked Rog what he wanted, and he clearly- for the first time in three days- said, "I want to get better!" Wow! My heart soared. That meant we could follow his desires and get him in for help. Priscilla helped me get him into the car. Thank you, Lord!

He was totally disoriented, dehydrated from refusing to eat or drink, and his potassium was deadly, at 6.6. It may have already caused a heart attack. We will know soon. Rog was angry with me for bringing him for a while, when they stabbed his neck to find a vein and it collapsed after all the pain. He was mad when they put in a catheter, and really upset when they put a hose in so he wouldn't have to sit on a potty all night while they got the potassium out of his body. But after a night of sleep he will get better and have his right mind again. He has forgiven me, he said.

He may want to die at home, but that is God's business. I am not having a hand in it, because I cannot handle that. I do not agree with active euthanasia because it makes a person murder another, and God tells us that is a grave sin. I may want it if I get in great pain, but that does not make it right. It really is an ethical dilemma today.

So for today, we can rest. If God takes him to heaven, we will be at peace, knowing we did not cause our beloved person to die early. If He chooses to answer our prayer for healing-since He says yes, no, or wait, we will rejoice big time!

Back to My Story

Why would anyone save such a record? Much energy has been invested to keep this dear man alive. I do not want a minute of it to go to waste. There is much to learn in this little book that may help us avoid it in our lives. I hope it was not a lot of suffering for nothing…but perhaps it was. Do you ever wonder why good men suffer this way? All I know is that he became a saint through the process. Is this the crucible that burns off the dross and exposes the gold? Evil men often escape such suffering until they leave the earth, but then theirs begins and lasts for all eternity. At least there was an end to Rog's tribulations.

Timing Is Everything

When we are in God's hands and His Spirit lives inside us, everything that happens is sifted through Him. He gives us favor (grace) in difficult times. Rog was healed many times and God gave him several miracles in the midst of his challenges. My dear husband has had over forty transfusions and his veins finally gave out a week ago. Blood tests were a nightmare every week, and near the end three times a day from a port in his arm. He was about to have a central line put in his neck for the second time when his body decided it had enough.

The disease process escalated with the new year of 2010. He spent a month in the hospital with fluid accumulation, countered by dehydration and constant blood loss and came home on full-time oxygen. He asked me to agree that he would not go to the hospital any more, meaning he was finished depending on doctors to fix the problems.

Please don't misunderstand. We had wonderful doctors that did all they knew to do, sometimes having to choose the least of two evils. They are not God and all humans have limitations. They had done all they could, except to try one more thing. They wanted to operate on his heart and give him two pig valves. He would not need Coumadin any more, but the price would be his kidneys, already failing. He chose not to do dialysis. His chance of survival during surgery was 50:50.

A home health nurse took Rog's blood pressure one day and it was falling drastically. Had we done nothing, he could have passed away peacefully at home. She asked him what he wanted. He said, "I want to get better." She said that meant another hospital visit, and he said OK. So she and I got him into my car and to Emergency, where he received more blood and fluids for dehydration. He was admitted once again. It was Monday, March 8.

Saturday morning I came to bring him home again and his bed was empty. My heart sunk! He had gone to ICU. A caretaker had fed him scrambled eggs, and unable even to swallow liquids at that point, he was too weak to chew them. He aspirated them, choking, and they spread all over his lungs. He was gone three minutes, and because he had been afraid to sign a "do not resuscitate" document, (DNR); the doctor brought him back to life and put in a ventilator.

He had to be sedated to handle the trauma. The doctor spent a half hour sucking eggs out of his lungs, but he still got aspiration pneumonia, in addition to a fungus infection and a urinary tract infection.

Eight days later, still on the ventilator, unable to breathe without it, he was alert now and then enough to shake his head yes or no. He did not yet want dialysis, did not want to be resuscitated if his heart stopped, and did NOT want that ventilator removed for sure, though it was wretched. The doctor had turned it off from time to time to test his ability to breathe and he failed miserably. I was urged to have the vent removed and let him go. Rog shook his head the best he could to indicate, "No!"

That evening, Saturday, March 20, Dave and Rob found him awake and wanting to stay that way while they visited, asking him yes or no questions. It was very special, and the most alert he had been since he choked.

We were told Rog would swell up from toxins and get confused before going into a coma. Then we would have to give an order to cut off his oxygen supply. God had mercy.

We obeyed what Rog wanted, and his heart stopped before he lost his senses. He had just started swelling, which actually gave his 120-pound frame a bit of filling out for his size 42 suit.

Graduation Day!

Tribute to Roger Emmett Parrott

As the editor and author of this book, I dedicate it to my precious husband, who passed away Sunday morning, March 21, 2010, after a violent but courageous battle against diabetes, kidney disease, anemia, and congestive heart failure. He left me behind to nurture a bunch of people, three sons and wives, eight grandkids and four and a half great grandkids. He won only because Jesus Christ lived in his heart and when his last enemy, death, tried to conquer him, Jesus took him home forever. Roger was a wonderful provider with great integrity, determination, and faith. We had a good life for 53 years, and I have no regrets. He worked his way up to become the Southern Operations Director of Herman Miller Furniture Company, and after 36 years, he retired, and passed on to heaven at 72. He was also the president of the North Fulton Chamber of Commerce for two years. He loved traveling, motorcycling, hunting, fishing, RV's...and later on, napping, napping.... and more napping.

Rog, with ticket in hand, caught the heavenly train Sunday morning at 9:39 AM. I saw him before he left, in a dream. He was in restraints, but figured a way to reach his ventilator and pull it out! He had been unable to breathe without it for eight days, and he found out he could breathe after yanking it out! He was running and talking and full of joy. I woke up and got dressed to go tell him about the dream. I figured it was God's way of showing me his miracle was on the way!

I got in the car, and remembered my cell phone back in the house. I ran back to get it and the phone rang. Deidre, the nurse, told me his heart was growing weak and irregular, and his blood pressure was falling. I drove the ten miles at record speed, but he left his body one-half a minute before I got in the room to say goodbye. He left without a struggle. He did everything he wanted to do in this life and he finally got his reward. We will rejoice for him and mourn our loss.

The funeral was at the Landmark Church, 3737 Holcomb Bridge Road, Norcross, 30092. We celebrated his homecoming with songs, testimonies, and a yummy dinner. His friends shared things at his funeral that shocked me. He had been such a great blessing to them in so many ways, but never boasted about it at all to me.

What a magnificent send-off! The church was never that full. I bought food for 150 and 200 people stayed for dinner. We ran out with the last plate! We are so blessed to have good friends and a precious family. All I can say is the entire experience was awesome beyond anything I could have imagined! Maybe it is because the nurse has her first day off in a very long time! I don't know what to do with myself...no pills to count, no painful toenails to trim, no lotion to rub in, and no nasty renal diet meals to fix and try to get him to eat. I don't need to test his blood and give him shots or urge him to eat, though I would have gladly waited on him every minute for just a little more time with him, but it was not fair to ask him to stay just for me.

Life is sweet and sour sauce, but for now it is just a great relief that nobody is shooting him with "life-giving" medicine, laying him flat letting him drown in his own fluids, or forcing air into his lungs while he tries to say his last words! Pure relief. The rest will come. I hope the joy continues to be my strength as it is right now! All is well with my soul. We fought a good fight and in the end we win no matter what.

He is safe in the arms of Jesus, and enjoying the reunion with those he loves. In no time we will reunite.

P.S. The timing of his departure amazes me. Our dear founding pastor returned to our church a week before. He had retired a few years before, but came back and took over to put it back together. Our friends Carol and Lonnie left Florida to go home to Minnesota just at the right time to be with me. My sister, brothers and spouses were able to be with us. My friend had cleaned my house for me the day before he died, which helped so much. People brought us enough food to feed the eight of us the entire time! Our cook at church had just lost his job and was free to make a wonderful dinner. The soundman was awaiting his first baby, and it did not come on the due date!

Rob had investigated funeral arrangements and had everything in order for us. Rog passed away after a busy limousine weekend of prom season so we had Rob's limos to carry us everywhere. Our dear founding pastor returned to the pulpit the week before, after being retired five years, to help the church get back on its feet. We could not have a funeral without this dear man. I asked friends in lieu of flowers to donate to Landmark Church in Norcross, and everyone was so generous to help us. Rog would have loved it.

My Best Friend

A month ago, I lost my best friend on earth. He looked a bit like Sean Connery and my psychology teacher, Bill Bloemendaal, or so I thought. He got more handsome as the years wore on, and I fell more in love with him as we both matured together. Just when it got as good as it can get, he got sick.

We had a good life, did everything a couple could dream of doing, got along as well as any two could, living in close proximity. He was as much a part of me as my right arm, and missing my right arm is quite a handicap. I will learn, however, over time, how to function without that arm, and life will again be exciting as ever it was.

I started out the process feeling downright giddy over the freedom from hospitals, oxygen tanks and sleepless nights. I had all my physical needs met, I could wander around the mall without hurrying home for some task, or without worrying that he was in the car waiting for me. I was grateful he was free of that awful ventilator down his throat keeping him from saying anything, and nobody was cutting on his neck to insert an IV because all his veins were collapsed.

Today is a new day, however. I watch a Sean Connery movie and tears flow. I realize just a bit, that Rog is not away on business or even in ICU any more. Last evening I went to the barn in a downpour to find the light on. Dave had come over to borrow the zero-turn tractor. He was just sitting on it with the engine running, and tears running down his face as he looked around at all Dad left behind. I, who had not wept much anymore by the time the sheet was drawn over his face, could not hold them back either. Michael is twelve, and decided we should get a grip, so he gave his little speech about Grandpa up there having a ball, and how soon we would be together again. He got all those words out before he broke down, too. Lila walked in and joined the pity party. What a sight to behold.

    Actually, I feel I am holding up fairly well. I am learning how to pay bills and run this place, repair things and hire help when needed. I replaced six RV tires and all the car tires and even took a short trip in the motor home without wrecking it. Life is so busy there is no time to grieve. I just seem to fall asleep throughout the day from time to time. It is so weird.

    I focus on Rog young and healthy, having a marvelous new life, seeing that everything I tried to get him to believe he now knows! He believed the most important things, so I know where he is today, and there is profound comfort in that. He was so courageous through several years of trials with diabetes and Coumadin, but it finally won. He fought our last enemy, death, and won eternally. We will meet again.

A Heartrending Letter from Rob's Wife

Hi Mom, 9/4/10

Thanks for the Michigan update. We sure do miss seeing everyone and can't wait to go back. Maybe some day soon.

I tried to read your story, but just can't now. I made it to where your journal picks up with all the sickness and Dad falling by the bathroom. Just miss him too much to read now.

Rob never talks about his dad but has told me how much he misses him and Chandler does, too. It is just too painful for Rob to share. His respect for you and Dad is not explainable. You two as parents instilled something in him that is remarkable. His love for his parents is truly what Christ intended.

Every night when I pray with Chandler we ask Jesus to give Poppy a hug and a kiss and tell him we love him. If we ever go to a restaurant and Chandler gets a balloon we always go outdoors and Chandler sends it to heaven with a kiss for Poppy. Chandler came up with that all by himself the morning Poppy went to Heaven. It has become the norm now to send all balloons to heaven. If that helps Chandler then it's okay!

Tears are apourin' now so no more about that. The only comfort I have is knowing he is with Jesus and would NEVER come back here if given a choice.

You know he was the only dad I ever really knew and I loved him so much. You know that day in ICU with the vent I was leaving and I told him, "I love you" and he mouthed through the vent, "I love you," and wiggled all his toes. Rob noticed and told me to "LOOK at his toes!" I knew it was okay for me to let him go.

I knew he loved me and would have wrapped his arms around me if he could, just like so many times at home when I was leaving. I am okay because I know I will see him again, but as for Chandler, my heart just breaks in two. He misses him so much. He still talks about Poppy and going to Poppy's and going places. Chandler cries for hours when Rob leaves because he thinks he is not coming back. This started around April of this year. I believe it is related to Poppy leaving. He just does not understand and it breaks my heart. Only God can give him comfort. I have been praying that the Lord will give him peace and let him understand in his own way. Love, Rhonda

What a Trip!

Rog had passed on to heaven. I had always wanted to drive the RV to California. After long deliberation, I finally made plans, found friends with adventurous spirits, and away we went. It was a glorious trip. I was so happy I had made the decision not to sell it. We saw Carlsbad Cavern and the Sonoma Desert and the Grand Canyon-we saw it all.

After a week and a half of sightseeing and immensely enjoying ourselves and each other's company, we arrived at our destination- the Pacific Ocean at Laguna Beach, California!

One evening, I parked the wonderful forty-foot motor home bulging with souvenirs and gifts for our families, and we ambled into a famous restaurant whose name I forget to celebrate our arrival. Supper was better than we could have imagined. When we were totally satiated with the stuff of this world we so enjoy, we left the restaurant and headed toward the RV, parked on a bluff on top of a low mountain overlooking the ocean.

We looked all around and couldn't locate the RV. I thought, *oh, no. Another senior moment! I can't remember where I parked it. And here we made it all the way to California with this scattered brain. What a miracle that was.*

It is never hard to find it, standing out like a train engine above all the other vehicles, but this time we couldn't spot it. It took me a few minutes to grasp the fact it was gone! Had someone stolen it? I had it locked. We started expressing all the possibilities. Finally it dawned on me that it could possibly have rolled down the mountain! Impossible as it seemed, it was the only realistic explanation, and it was time to check it out.

As God would have it, two men in a wrecker were within our vision, working to get a car hauled away from the parking lot. I ran over to them and told them our predicament. I was hoping they would let me ride in their wrecker down the mountain to find it, hopefully resting on an uphill slope nearby. No such luck. They took two bicycles off the back of the wrecker and headed downward, with me running frantically behind them while the girls stood waiting and praying on the former parking spot of the RV.

As I ran, I was watching for signs the RV had hit anything, but there was not a clue anywhere, and no frantic people were around screaming about a runaway motor home flying through their neighborhood. I hoped God had put it in a safe place and I'd find it waiting patiently for me to find it.

I stopped to catch my breath from time to time and talked with dog-walkers and such, but nobody had a clue. As I got closer to the bottom, I realized it was a gradual winding road going toward the beach, but there was not one rise in the entire road. How in the world could that big monster make it to the bottom? The road was banked, but still…I was so confused…and terrified that someone could have easily been killed!

It seemed like it was a mile to the ocean. The men made it down quickly, but it took me a while. As the road straightened out and the beach was before me, from high above the water, I saw what I had hoped I would never see.

There was the very top of the RV, satellite dish glowing in the sunset, skylights I rarely had seen, and the entire motor home was underwater! I couldn't even think. I sat in the middle of the road in shock. People were standing nearby just staring at it, and the wrecker men just shook their heads.

I thought, *Oh my. I guess I should have sold it after all. Too late now!* Going through my mind was the incredible task of drying it out. Could it be salvaged at all? I had three hundred recently published books in there I hadn't even distributed yet. All our gifts were in there. And the comfy mattress on that king-sized bed! I could never dry that out! Would it ever run? And how in the world could a wrecker even pull it out? I wondered if by some miracle it was airtight enough to be dry inside. Nothing is impossible with God. After all, if He could get it safely down that mountain, anything was possible.

Then instead of weeping, I got into hysterical laughing. *Rog is in heaven, and he can't yell at me. I have good insurance that will cover it all, and God took care of the difficult decision I was trying to make about parting with it. The decision was made. All is well that ends well. What I had considered a tragedy was just another amazing moment in my life. Who will ever believe this one?*

Then I woke up. Wow, what a dream that was!

Journal 2012-2015

How are we doing without Rog?

My son Tom and his girlfriend were asleep in his old car in October of 2013 with no place to go. I asked God what to do. I had tried this once or twice before and he always returned to her and of course went back on heroin with her. Big risk. Drugs were a problem in his life off and on since he was thirteen! God had let me know, however, they would be coming for the last time. When I asked what to do, He just said, "WWJD?" (What would Jesus do?)

So I took them in and fed them breakfast. She weighed 108 pounds at five foot seven! He was just a dead man walking weighing around 120.

They promised to go to rehab in a week and pleaded with me to help them detox first, which rehab centers require. They gave me their credit cards, food stamp card, and car keys. I locked up all my stuff, put a code on the computer, and put my phone in my locked bedroom-padlocked. I fed them, got them nausea meds, Gatorade and everything I could find. Tom was very sick for a week, mostly PTSD, I think. (Post-traumatic stress disorder.)

She never got sick at all! It was quite a miracle, since tests had proven they had both taken the same amount of drugs together. My mind could not relax thinking she may have been sneaking a drug. But after several amazing miracles I realized God had delivered her supernaturally. Thank God! I couldn't handle them both so sick.

They got married on Halloween after being together twelve years! My precious pastors, Jeanette and Fred Kelly, quickly got together some witnesses, and even bought a cake. They were happy to obey God, and He honored their obedience.

I never left them and if I went they went with me. We went to church a lot, and watched only Christian TV. They got a good education that is still continuing. Stephanie is soaking up Christianity faster than anyone I have ever seen. Her faith is growing daily. I fed them so good they each gained 30 pounds in a month!

God said to me, *The foundation is coming along nicely. (Yes, not everyone believes God can talk to us, but this is not a new concept. Study the Word.)*

The other night I cooked a turkey for church and there they both were at the oven- eleven PM- waiting anxiously for it to come out. They begged for some turkey. (That is a treat?) They gobbled it down like starving pilgrims! I said, "My, you were deprived!"

Tom said, "Mom, you have no idea! Where we lived Steph was the only ones with food stamps and the other druggies living there got up in the night and ate up all our food! Then they denied it all." This victorious touching story will soon be published, called, "Quicksand."

Tom went to Teen Challenge Dec. 31. Nobody would take her because of her wheelchair and Multiple Sclerosis. We rented a room for her to stay with a Christian woman and I took off for Florida Jan. 1. I really needed a break!

Tom left Teen Challenge after only two months, but had some good reasons so I didn't fight it. I flew them both to Florida for a week, so he could repair my RV and drive home with me. It went great. They came to me healthy! Happy! Giddy with joy!

My son Rob found a little house for them to rent three miles away. I keep an eye on them, but they are now on their own! Tom is fixing cars. He is a great Mercedes technician. Stephanie has just been admitted to physical therapy and will learn to walk again. The doctor would not support her much while an addict but he is very encouraged now. God is so good!

Dave started a used car business and is a born salesman. Rob is a gifted car painter and mechanic. They are all hard workers.

Rog left me with good training and life skills. I am independent and at peace. I try to keep God in first place where He belongs in my life. Sometimes I admit writing gets in the way, but I find my way back to Him.

As I write in March 2015, Stephanie just had an MRI that reveals all the lesions in her brain have disappeared! She has a few left in her spine. We expect God is doing this in steps. Praise His wonderful name! Life is good! Amen.

Unique and fascinating books by Judy Parrott are available new and used on Amazon.com and Kindle.com:

"Break Every Chain"

Addiction Recovery Stories

Judy Parrott shares personal experiences of deliverance, emotional healing and salvation with addicted family members who now walk in freedom, joyfully fulfilling God's plan for their lives.

Testimonies of victory from every addiction will encourage you, with a complete set of easy pain-free recovery tools from God, the Deliverer. Her background includes nursing, seminary, publishing several books about miracles, and nurturing a family of eight grandchildren and five great grandkids. She is a widow who chooses to serve God above all.

"Mysterious Wonders"

Miracles started happening to me nearly every day forty years ago when I became a

Christian. I thought it was normal until I spoke with other believers who claimed they no longer occur. They told me after the last apostle died, the gifts were no longer available. It shook me up, and I realized this belief is common but totally incorrect. This book of miracles is evidence of God's supernatural intervention and His plan for the church. None are exaggerated or untrue, and most are documented, though that is not necessary. The proof is in the pudding, as they say.

"Supernatural Events from God"

This is a record of the natural flow of the supernatural among us. Miracles, signs and wonders are God's hugs. Read about salvation, deliverance, miracles, dreams, visions and angelic visitations.

"A Life Worth Living...the Second One"

Autobiography of a life transformed by supernatural revelations. Family stories, miracles, angelic visitations, healings, astounding answers to prayer, the traumas of life and victories that overcame them. You can relate, I promise. Entertaining variety that teaches life lessons in the process.

Reviews are greatly appreciated!

CMA rally in Arkansas. Rog is second.

Left to right: Tom, Rob, Judy and Dave

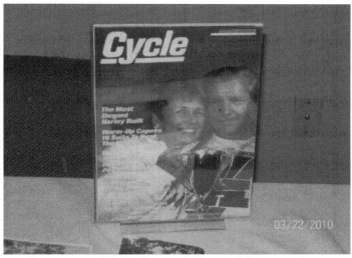

Impressed? Judy and Rog. Cute, huh?

Supplement for those who like to keep reading!

Thoughts to Ponder About Medical Events

After all we had gone through I wondered if our total trust in the medical profession is the best thing for us or not. I believe we need moderation in all things, including putting our health completely in the hands of others. The Bible says that King Asa went to the physicians and died. What does that mean? It also says that a woman spent all she had on physicians, and they were unable to help her. It says that cursed is the man who puts his trust in man. And it says to put God first.

Now I go to the doctor if I have a problem, but I certainly pray first, and wait on God, and try to do what I can before going. I believe God has gifted doctors greatly, and when God works with a doctor, he can help a great deal. I still read a lot and learn what I can about the procedures and medications. Sometimes I decide not to take certain measures. It is not that I disagree with them, but may not be always willing to take certain risks.

The Bible is our life's manual, and our wisdom comes from God, who inspired everything in the Bible for a purpose. In the name of man's imperfect wisdom, we have done many foolish things. As a child, I was allowed to play with radioactivity. A delightful invention was at my disposal called an ex-ray machine. It was in the shoe store. While my brother and Dad were buying shoes, I was busy pressing a button with my foot in the machine as long as I liked. It was fun to see my bones through my shoe. Today such great exposure is unthinkable due to increased knowledge about radiation and cancer.

I recall an assignment in nursing school. I had to evaluate the effect of medicines on a single patient of my choosing. I chose to use my father as the guinea pig. Dad was taking over twenty powerful but tiny pills a day.

As I studied the side effects of each on the other, I realized why he was in such torment! He was so weary; he could hardly stay awake some days. He was depressed most of the time, and was up several times every night to urinate, because his doctor had prescribed a strong diuretic "to be taken at bedtime"! (Why at bedtime?)

His blood pressure medicine had lowered his pressure to such an extent he was dizzy most of the time, and he sometimes fell down if he got out of bed without sitting a few minutes.

He had been on thyroid medicine for an underactive thyroid for several years. He was told he would be on it for life. Well, he went to a new doctor, who took one test on his blood, and removed it. (Some test results can be up to 30% inaccurate. If drastic, they should be redone, but often insurance will not pay for it.) Dad began gaining an enormous amount of weight, his hair fell out by the handfuls, his limbs were cold, and he had to begin sleeping with socks on his icy cold feet and on his hands as well! These are all symptoms of hypothyroidism. The doctor ignored his complaints. He depended on the test results, which usually makes sense.

I handed my evaluation in to my instructor, who was very alarmed at my findings. Dad subsequently changed doctors, and was taken off half of the twenty medications.

Another thing that causes me to be cautious about putting my life in another's hands results from the birth of a baby.

Our son Tom and his wife Laurie had a baby, born with major malformations. She was diagnosed with a VADER syndrome, a defect of the twenty-first chromosome called Trisomy twenty-one.

At birth, she had a missing forearm, a large hole between her heart chambers, an esophagus that did not connect to her stomach, but to her lungs, and many other anomalies. Surgery was successful on her esophagus, but she remained on oxygen with tube feedings.

The parents were told she would not survive, and to please sign a consent form to remove life support, which they did. Of course, the grandparents were expecting a miracle! We were informed she would pass away in a few moments, and to make proper arrangements.

We waited anxiously for the report. It never came! The oxygen was removed, and she continued to thrive! The nurses were very amazed. A few days later she was released to go home. The parents stayed with us, and we took shifts watching over little Robin Amber. She weighed about four pounds. We still had to feed her through a stomach tube, and were unable to lay her flat due to the heart defect. But we were thrilled to see her alive, and knew God had a plan.

A few weeks later, her two year old brother got sick with a bad cold and flu. We were confined at the time to one room, as an ice storm had cut off the electricity. We had the fireplace going for heat. The next day, little Robin had pneumonia, and was admitted to the hospital.

The third day of her hospitalization, a nurse called me to tell me that she could lose her job for calling, but that the baby was on orders not to be fed anything. For three days, she had been crying and had not been fed!

The nurse could not stand the injustice of it, and had to let us know! We rushed to the hospital, but a half hour after the call, Robin had passed away. The hospital was legally protected because of the permission slip her parents had signed several weeks before. Robin Amber lived one month and went to heaven, one year almost to the day before her brother Matthew was born.

Do I sign any permission slips? No, I surely don't. I don't even offer my organs on my driver's license. My family has permission to give them away when I leave, but I am not giving the public the right to do as they wish with them.

Dear, dear Judy.
My heart just aches for you!! I understand the dilemma you're in. Rog wants to die at home when the time comes (sort of like he'll be in charge that way), but you cannot be complicit in his death. The question I have is this. *Is it euthanasia if he simply dies the way our ancestors did, without the extraordinary measures that are available now?* I don't know (only God does for sure)—but I think perhaps not.

And then there's the statement he made that he wants to get better! As long as he knows the Lord, it's a win-win situation, right? But as illness continues, how much longer will he want to recover? I guess only time will tell that one.

I want to share something with you. I have no idea if it will help in any way, it's just the telling of an experience that you may compare with your own or not, as it fits. An aunt is very different from a husband. I don't claim to have any answers, but I've experienced the question of "Oh, Lord! What have I done!?"

In June of 2004, my little auntie who was then ninety-four years old developed a diffuse abdominal tumor that mercilessly ate up her organs. She hadn't been feeling well since December but we thought it might be part of the gift of being extremely old. She had a powerful zest for living and until late May, didn't let feeling rotten slow her down. Then she crashed on Memorial Day weekend, and died on June 8th. Her PCP later told me she thought the tumor could have originated between three and six months earlier in one of the kidneys, then just spread from right to left until pretty much nothing was left in its path.

My aunt was a retired RN, a nursing supervisor in the same hospital where she died, and deep down I think she knew something was seriously amiss, much more than being extremely old.

My cousin was the one who made all her medical decisions. She lived five hours closer and saw her more frequently than I did. She wasn't around the night I stayed in the hospital room with Auntie, who knew she was dying, was in terrible pain and couldn't sleep. Her Fentanyl patch wasn't working, even when a fresh one was applied. The nurse told her she had an order for morphine. Aunt Alice said to me, "I don't know what to do. What should I do, El?"

"I can't make the decision for you, Auntie. But I *can* ask you a question: It's three in the morning. What do you want more than anything else in the world right now?"

We'd already settled the question of Heaven. Earlier that day, she had literally experienced a deathbed conversion and it was as real as anything I ever saw in any church or at any altar. So she wasn't afraid to die, she just didn't particularly want to.

She thought for a moment and then she said, "I want to sleep, El. More than anything in the world, I just want to get some sleep."

"Okay. I think we both know there's only one way that's going to happen. Can you sleep *without* morphine?"

She frowned and thought again. "I don't think so, no."

"Okay. Do you want me to call your nurse?"

"Yes."

"Are you *sure*, Auntie? This has to be your decision, not mine."

"Yes." She had an order for two milligrams. She asked for only one and it was slipped into her IV. I was holding her hand. But then my particular little hell began because suddenly, she froze in position. She was asleep, no doubt about that! She'd drawn her knees up high because she was in so much pain, and it took about eight hours for them to relax and drop down so she was in a normal sleep position. She never regained consciousness—and she surely never felt any more pain. She died peacefully three mornings later.

I struggled with that for months and to a degree, it still haunts me. When her little body froze, I felt as if one very large hand was clutching my innards and squeezing them, and another was doing the same thing to my throat. Although her nurse said it was a normal reaction, I thought for sure I had helped kill her.

But now with the perspective of six years I have peace about it and I have had for some time. I don't believe the shot killed her; I believe cancer did, and I believe she had a much easier death than she would have if she'd been fully conscious and in uncontrollable pain.

My gut—which isn't the gut that counts!!—tells me that if Rog is not in a lot of pain when he dips down, if prolonging his life with extraordinary measures will ensure that he *is* in pain—while indeed he may live longer—my gut says that simply stopping the "extras" (feeding tubes, IVs, resuscitation, needlesneedlesneedles, etc.) is not the same thing as euthanasia—where a deliberate *effort* is made to end a life. Letting him go when the time comes normally isn't euthanizing him.

I hope I haven't added to your struggle, Judy. If you ever want to talk and just vent or have someone to pray with you, please call me, okay? And be very sure of our prayers.

Love, Elin

Dear Judy,
From the year I worked on the pediatrics floor at St. Vincent's Hospital in Worcester, I remember only two kids clearly. One was a little girl with failure to thrive for her diagnosis and the other was a baby named Steven, who had the just tiniest little blister in the crease behind his knee the day he was born. It looked so *innocent*—but it spelled death. He - was - *beautiful*! And I am still haunted by his eyes. On rare occasions I'll see a baby with that same expression on his or her little face and think, "Oh, Lord, please no. Those are *Steven's* eyes!" He had Epidermolysis Bullosa, an exceedingly rare (mercifully!) condition that has no cure. His parents were wailing with grief the day he was born.

At first they came to see him every day, but then they couldn't stand to see his suffering.

At the end, just about three months, there were only two people who would visit with him. One was the nurse's aide who tended him (I was always convinced it was because *someone* had to and she was chosen because of her low rank: it certainly wasn't because she wanted to be!) and I was the other. I called him Stevie and used to get my secretarial work done as quickly as possible and then go in and sit by his isolette. I couldn't touch him because it would have been far too painful for him. But he and I would lock eyes and I'd read or sing to him, usually *Jesus Loves Me* or something else I could turn into a lullaby. I never saw him smile; really, did he have reason? But at least he wasn't denied the dignity of having someone make eye contact with him.

It broke my heart when that baby died. And yes, he was alone that night. He weighed in at nine pounds; he weighed out at less than six. Now usually, I can look at someone who is truly dying what I consider "early" and think, I wonder what the Lord has spared him by taking him so soon. But it's really hard to do that when I think of Steven.

There are hard questions and some have no answers that we will see before we die. All we can do is trust Him with it all.

Must dash for now. I'll send you a brief story tomorrow to give you a laugh. Elin Lee

Letter from a Nurse Friend

Judy, you will soon find that I am opinionated, if nothing else. I read your article and I have some thoughts.

If you have read any Francis Schaffer you know why doctors are leaning toward death these days. When the Supreme Court legalized abortion our society then started to believe that there can be a life not worthy to be lived and we as finite people get to decide who that is. Nonsense!! Life is sacred and we have no right to pretend to be a god.

However, I am strongly in favor of Western medicine performed by a TRUSTED doctor. The point of Western medicine is RESEARCH. They perform tests over and over and get the same results. That means they are sure of that fact and then can go on to another. We live in a sinful world that suffers the consequences of sin.

Romans 1 talks about the "wrath of God is revealed from heaven against all unrighteousness". I believe the reason for sickness and death is sin in the world. But, when God created the world, he gave us a mandate. In fact, it is called the Creation Mandate. We are to conquer the earth and subdue it. Gen 1:28. The theologians who came after the reformation taught that we could still carry out this mandate. Our relationship with God is restored through redemption, our ability to conquer nature for our use is accomplished by means of science.

I think our country has come closer than any in fulfilling that mandate. We have prolonged life and developed much technology that makes life easier and more pleasant. I think that was God's design. When my dad was born the average life span for a man was 53.

While we have not perfectly overcome death and disease, we have made great progress sustaining life. It is sacred and should be valued and prolonged. We must use good judgment about the doctors we use to help us evaluate the side effects of medications and procedures. Altering the chemistry of our bodies does have side effects and cannot be taken lightly. But, yes, Western medicine backed up by research can prolong life. That is a good thing. I hope I have given you some things to think about.   Cindy

I am grateful there are doctors and nurses. I know they do very useful things, and God uses them a great deal to save lives. Sometimes we need human intervention, led by God's spirit. They are not God, however, and they cannot be a substitute for Him. He can use them, and if necessary He can do things without them- if we are sold out to Him! If not – God help us!

Dying and death

When kidney failure reaches the stage where dialysis or transplantation is required, refusing such treatment means that the patient will die. This could happen within a few days or weeks, depending on how much kidney function they still have. A patient may decide to explore the option of refusing treatment. It is the responsibility of the medical team to counsel such patients and their families, and support them in their decision.

Some patients may decide to try dialysis for a few weeks or months. This allows them to evaluate both the good and bad sides of life on dialysis, and to make an informed choice. It may also give patients time to settle their affairs and resolve conflicts, or have time to say goodbye to family members who live abroad.

Deciding not to start dialysis

There may be good medical as well as personal reasons not to dialyze. The opportunity of refusing dialysis can be a blessing in disguise for someone with an inoperable cancer, for instance.

Withdrawal from dialysis is not an uncommon cause of death in long-standing kidney patients, particularly those who are elderly.

A patient who decides not to have any treatment, or to cease treatment after it has started, will receive counseling and support. The medical team will discuss the implications of the patient's decision at length with both patient and his or her family.

The medical team will support the patient's decision as long as they are sure that it is a fully informed choice. It is a good idea for patients to let relatives and doctors know their wishes should they become unable to make the choice themselves. This could happen if the patient is unconscious following a stroke, or otherwise mentally unfit to decide.

Sometimes patients refuse treatment, but then change their mind. This is perfectly understandable and acceptable. Any patient has the right to change his or her mind at any time.

It is helpful for some patients who feel they do not want dialysis, to agree to a trial of treatment. This allows them to see what is involved before making a final decision.

The medical team will give appropriate medication to a patient who refuses treatment or decides to cease treatment. This will keep the patient comfortable and free from pain until death. The team will provide support to the patient and their family throughout this time. If the patient chooses to go home to die, the renal team will also refer the patient and family to community-based agencies that will be able to provide them with support and comfort.

Informed choice

Some patients—those with Alzheimer's disease, for instance—may not be able to make an informed choice about treatment. It can be helpful if patients make their wishes known at a time when they are able to decide for themselves.

Withdrawing from treatment after transplant

While successful transplantation offers the best possible quality of life for a patient with kidney failure, it is not without risks. The powerful drugs used to prevent rejection can lead to infections and to cancers, including serious cancers such as lymphoma.

One of the treatments for lymphoma is to stop or reduce the immunosuppressant drugs. In this case, the kidney will be rejected and the patient will need to go back on dialysis.

The advantage of being on dialysis is that the patient can choose when he or she has had enough, and decide to withdraw.
Other patients, who have had a long period of successful transplantation, develop an incurable condition unrelated to the drugs they are taking. One option might be to stop taking their immunosuppressant and allow the kidney to fail. Then they could die from kidney failure without dialysis.

Death from kidney failure

On average, patients who are passing reasonable amounts of urine can survive for 2 to 6 weeks with untreated end-stage kidney failure. Patients who are passing little or no urine can survive for 10 to 14 days.

The symptoms that may need to be controlled in the final days before death from kidney failure include nausea, muscle twitching, and breathlessness. Sometimes there is some agitation and confusion. Pain is not usually a serious problem.

If a patient wishes to die at home, specialist nursing can usually be arranged. Some hospices will admit kidney patients who have decided not to dialyze. Hospice care is designed to take into account the needs and feelings of both patients and family.

Most renal units are experienced in the care of dying patients, who are usually nursed in quiet and privacy.

One of the benefits of remaining in hospital is that if the patient decides to accept dialysis after all, the facilities are close at hand.

From the Internet

I believe God uses miracles as a dinner bell to call His children to the table. Jesus is coming soon, and he is getting our attention. Mark 16 was given for us today, the last words of Jesus Christ before He ascended into heaven. He will return the same way He left. Get ready!

The End

Heavens Hands Publications ©

This is a blank page. Enjoy!

Made in the USA
Columbia, SC
04 May 2023